The Inner Nature of Music
and
the Experience of Tone

Selected lectures from the work of

Rudolf Steiner

The Inner Nature of Music
and
the Experience of Tone

Selected lectures from the work of

Rudolf Steiner

ANTHROPOSOPHIC PRESS

Cover produced with funding assistance from the
Cultural Freedom Fund.

The lectures appearing here were published in the
German volume, *Das Wesen des Musikalischen und
das Tonerlebnis im Menschen*, Rudolf Steiner Ver-
lag, Dornach. They were translated from the German by Maria St. Goar and edited by Alice Wulsin.

10 9 8 7 6 5 4 3

Cover design by Van James

Library of Congress Cataloging in Publication Data

Steiner, Rudolf, 1861–1925.
   The inner nature of music and the experience of tone.

   Translated selections from: Das Wesen des Musikalischen
und das Tonerlebnis im Menschen.
   1. Music—Philosophy and aesthetics.   2.   Anthroposophy.
I.   Wulsin, Alice.   II.   Title.
ML3800.S8613   1983   780'.1   83-45952
ISBN 0-88010-074-5 (pbk.)
ISBN 0-88010-055-9

Printed in the United States of America

Table of Contents

Foreword

This volume contains the only two sets of lectures that Rudolf Steiner gave primarily on musical subjects. The first group of three lectures, given in 1906, explains why music has always held a special position among the arts. Music is the only art form whose archetypal origin is in the spiritual rather than in the physical world, as is the case with architecture, sculpture, or painting. Since every night during sleep man's soul lives in the spiritual world—essentially a light-filled ocean of sounds—it is understandable why music speaks so directly and powerfully to almost everyone. The creative musician translates what he has experienced in the spiritual world into harmonies, melodies, and rhythms of music that is physically manifest. Music, therefore, is a messenger from the spiritual world, speaking to us through tones as long as we are unable to partake in supersensible events directly.

In the remaining lectures, given in 1922–23, Steiner discusses man and his experience of the world of tones, an experience that has undergone profound changes during the course of evolution. Before the Atlantean catastrophe, described in detail in Steiner's *An Outline of Occult Science*, man perceived only those intervals that were larger than the seventh; such intervals lifted him outside his body and made any musical experience a cosmic-spiritual one. In the early post-Atlantean period man's experience of the interval narrowed to that of the fifth; in our modern age, the period of the experience of the third, we now perceive the fifth to be empty. This feeling of emptiness actually is caused, as Steiner explains, by the withdrawal of the gods from man.

An extensive course for singers and other practicing musicians planned for the later part of the year 1924 could not take place due to the onset of Rudolf Steiner's mortal illness. The only other lecture cycle musicians can turn to is the tone eurythmy course, given in Dornach in February 1924 and published as *Eurythmy as Visible Music*. The collection of lectures presented here is thus an unusual treasure.

Erika V. Asten

I

For those who care to reflect on it, music has always been something of an enigma from the aesthetic point of view. On the one hand, music is most readily comprehensible to the soul, to the immediately sensitive realm of human feeling (*Gemüt*); on the other hand, it also presents difficulties for those wishing to grasp its effects. If we wish to compare music with the other arts, we must say that all the others actually have models in the physical world. When a sculptor creates a statue of Apollo or Zeus, for example, he works from the idealized reality of the human world. The same is true of painting, in which today (1906) only an immediate impression of reality is considered valid. In poetry also an attempt is made to create a copy of reality. One who wished to apply this approach to music, however, would arrive at scarcely any results at all. Man must ask himself what the origin is of the artistically formed tones and what they are related to in the world.

Schopenhauer, a luminary of the nineteenth century, brought clear and well-defined ideas to bear on art. He placed music in an unique position among the arts and held that art possessed a particular value for the life of man. At the foundation of his philosophy, as its leitmotif, is the tenet: Life is a disagreeable affair; I attempt to make it bearable by reflecting on it. According to Schopenhauer, a blind, unconscious will rules the entire world. It forms the stones, then brings forth plants from

1

the stones, and so on, because it is always discontent. A yearning for the higher thus dwells in everything.

Human beings sense this, though with greatly varying intensity. The savage who lives in dim consciousness feels the discontent of the will much less than a civilized human being, who can experience the pain of existence much more keenly. Schopenhauer goes on to say that the mental image or idea (*Vorstellung*) is a second aspect that man knows in addition to the will. It is like a Fata Morgana, a misty form or a ripple of waves in which the images of the will—this blind, dark urge—mirror themselves. The will reaches up to this phantom-image in man. When he becomes aware of the will, man becomes even more discontent. There are means, however, by which man can achieve a kind of deliverance from the blind urge of the will. One of these is art. Through art man is able to raise himself above the discontent of will.

When a person creates a work of art, he creates out of his mental image. While other mental images are merely pictures, however, it is different in the case of art. The Zeus by Phidias, for instance, was not created by copying an actual man. Here, the artist combined many impressions; he retained in his memory all the assets and discarded all the faults. He formed an archetype from many human beings, which can be embodied nowhere in nature; its features are divided among many individuals. Schopenhauer says that the true artist reproduces the archetypes—not the mental images that man normally has, which are like copies, but the archetypes. By proceeding to the depths of creative nature, as it were, man attains deliverance.

This is the case with all the arts except music. The other arts must pass through the mental image, and they therefore render up pictures of the will. Tone, however, is a direct expression of the will itself, without interpola-

2

tion of the mental image. When man is artistically engaged with tone, he puts his ear to the very heart of nature itself; he perceives the will of nature and reproduces it in series of tones. In this way, according to Schopenhauer, man stands in an intimate relationship to the Thing-in-Itself and penetrates to the innermost essence of things. Because man feels himself near to this essence in music, he feels a deep contentment in music.

Out of an instinctive knowledge, Schopenhauer attributed to music the role of directly portraying the very essence of the cosmos. He had a kind of instinctive presentiment of the actual situation. The reason that the musical element can speak to everyone, that it affects the human being from earliest childhood, becomes comprehensible to us from the realm of existence in which music has its true prototypes.

When the musician composes, he cannot imitate anything. He must draw the motifs of the musical creation out of his soul. We will discover their origin by pointing to worlds that are imperceptible to the senses. We must consider how these higher worlds are actually constituted. Man is capable of awakening higher faculties of the soul that ordinarily slumber. Just as the physical world is made visible to a blind person following an operation to restore his sight, so the inner soul organs of man can also be awakened in order that he might discern the higher spiritual worlds.

When man develops these faculties that otherwise slumber, when, through meditation, concentration, and so forth, he begins to develop his soul, he ascends step by step. The first thing he experiences is a peculiar transformation of his dream world. When, during meditation, man is able to exclude all memories and experiences of the outer sense world and yet can retain a soul content, his dream world begins to acquire a great regularity.

Then, when he awakens in the morning, it feels as if he arose out of a flowing cosmic ocean. He knows that he has experienced something new. It is as if he emerged from an ocean of light and colors unlike anything he has known in the physical world. His dream experiences gain increasing clarity. He recalls that in this world of light and color there were things and beings that distinguished themselves from those of the ordinary world in that one could penetrate them; they did not offer resistance. Man becomes acquainted with a number of beings whose element, whose body, consists of colors. They are beings who reveal and embody themselves in color. Gradually, man expands his consciousness throughout that world and, upon awakening, recalls that he had taken part in that realm. His next step is to take that world with him into the daily world. Man gradually learns to see what is called the astral body of the human being. He experiences a world that is much more real than the ordinary, physical world. The physical world is a kind of condensation that has been crystallized out of the astral world. In this way, man now has two levels of consciousness, the everyday waking consciousness and the dream consciousness.

Man attains a still higher stage when he is able to transform the completely unconscious state of sleep into one of consciousness. The student on the path of spiritual training learns to acquire continuity of consciousness for a part of the night, for that part of the night that does not belong to the dream life but that is wholly unconscious. He now learns to be conscious in a world about which he formerly knew nothing. This new world is not one of light and colors but announces itself first as a world of tone. In this state of consciousness, man develops the faculty to hear spiritually and to perceive tone combinations and varieties of tone inaudible to the physical ear. This world is called Devachan.

Now, one should not believe that when man hears the

4

world of tone welling up he does not retain the world of light and colors as well. The world of tone is permeated also with the light and colors that belong to the astral world. The most characteristic element of the Devachanic world, however, is this flowing ocean of tones. From this world of the continuity of consciousness, man can bring the tone element down with him and thus hear the tone element in the physical world. A tone lies at the foundation of everything in the physical world. Each aspect of the physical represents certain Devachanic tones. All objects have a spiritual tone at the foundation of their being, and, in his deepest nature, man himself is such a spiritual tone. On this basis, Paracelsus said, "The realms of nature are the letters, and man is the word that is composed of these letters."

Each time the human being falls asleep and loses consciousness, his astral body emerges from his physical body. In this state man is certainly unconscious but living in the spiritual world. The spiritual sounds make an impression on his soul. The human being awakens each morning from a world of the music of the spheres, and from this region of harmony he re-enters the physical world. If it is true that man's soul experiences Devachan between two incarnations on earth, then we may also say that during the night the soul feasts and lives in flowing tone, as the element from which it is actually woven and which is the soul's true home.

The creative musician transposes the rhythm, the harmonies, and the melodies that impress themselves on his etheric body during the night into physical tone. Unconsciously the musician has received the musical prototype from the spiritual world, which he then transposes into physical sounds. This is the mysterious relationship between music that resounds here in the physical world and hearing spiritual music during the night.

When a person is illuminated by light, he casts a

shadow on the wall. The shadow is not the actual person. In the same way, music produced in the physical world is a shadow, a real shadow of the much loftier music of Devachan. The archetype, the pattern, of music exists in Devachan, and physical music is but a reflection of the spiritual reality.

Now that we have made this clear, we will try to grasp the effect of music on the human being. This is the configuration of the human being that forms the basis of esoteric investigation: physical body, etheric body, astral body, and ego or "I." The etheric body is an etheric archetype of the physical body. A much more delicate body, which is related to the etheric body and inclines toward the astral realm, is the sentient body [*Empfindungsleib*]. Within these three levels of the body we see the soul. The soul is the most closely connected with the sentient body. The sentient soul[1] is incorporated, as it were, into the sentient body; it is placed within the sentient body. Just as a sword forms a whole with the scabbard into which it is placed, so the sentient body and the sentient soul represent a whole. In addition to these, man also possesses a feeling or intellectual soul [*Gemüts- oder Verstandesseele*] and, as a still higher member, the consciousness soul. The latter is connected with Manas, or spirit self.[2] When the human being is asleep, the sentient body remains in bed with the physical and etheric bodies, but the higher soul members, including the sentient soul, dwell in the world of Devachan.

In physical space we feel all other beings as outside of us. In Devachan, however, we do not feel ourselves outside of other beings; instead, they permeate us, and we are within them as well. Therefore, in all esoteric schools, the sphere of Devachan and also the astral realm have been called "the world of permeability."

When man lives and weaves in the world of flowing

tones, he himself is saturated by these tones. When he returns from the Devachanic world, his own consciousness soul, intellectual soul, and sentient soul are permeated with the vibrations of the Devachanic realm; he has these within himself, and with them he penetrates the physical world. When man has absorbed these vibrations, they enable him to work from his sentient soul onto the sentient body and the etheric body. Having brought these vibrations of Devachan along with him, man can convey them to his etheric body, which then resonates with these vibrations. The nature of the etheric and the sentient bodies is based on the same elements, on spiritual tone and spiritual vibrations. The etheric body is lower than the astral body, but the activity exercised in the etheric body stands higher than the activity of the astral body. Man's evolution consists of his transforming with his "I" the bodies he possesses: first, the astral body is transformed into Manas (spirit self), then the etheric body into Buddhi (life spirit), and finally the physical body into Atma (spirit man). Since the astral body is the most delicate, man requires the least force to work on it. The force needed to work on the etheric body must be acquired from the Devachanic world, and the force man needs for the transformation of the physical body must be attained from the higher Devachanic world. One can work on the astral body with the forces of the astral world itself, but the etheric body requires the forces of the Devachanic world. One can work on the physical body only with the forces of the still higher Devachanic world.

During the night, from the world of flowing tones, man receives the force he needs to communicate these sounds to his sentient body and his etheric body. A person is musically creative or sensitive to music because these sounds are present already in his sentient body. Although man is unaware of having absorbed tones during the

7

night, when he awakens in the morning, he nevertheless
senses these imprints of the spiritual world within him
when he listens to music. When he hears music, a clairvoyant can perceive how the tones flow, how they seize
the more solid substance of the etheric body and cause it
to reverberate. From this reverberation a person experiences pleasure, because he feels like a victor over his
etheric body by means of his astral body. This pleasurable
feeling is strongest when a person is able to overcome
what is already in his etheric body.

The etheric body continuously resounds in the astral
body. When a person hears music, the impression is experienced first in the astral body. Then, the tones are consciously sent to the etheric body, and man overcomes the
tones already there. This is the basis both of the pleasure
of listening to music and of musical creativity.

Along with certain musical sounds, something of the
astral body flows into the etheric body. The latter now
has received new tones. A kind of struggle arises between
the sentient body and the etheric body. If these tones are
strong enough to overcome the etheric body's own tones,
cheerful music in the major key results. When music is in
a major key, one can observe how the sentient body is the
victor over the etheric body. In the case of minor keys,
the etheric body has been victor over the sentient body;
the etheric body has opposed the vibrations of the sentient body.

When man dwells within the musical element, he lives
in a reflection of his spiritual home. In this shadow image
of the spiritual, the human soul finds its highest exaltation, the most intimate connection with the primeval element of man. This is why even the most humble soul is so
deeply affected by music. The most humble soul feels in
music an echo of what it has experienced in Devachan.
The soul feels at home there. Each time he listens to
music man senses, "Yes, I am from another world!"

From an intuitive knowledge of this Schopenhauer assigned the central position among the arts to music, and he said that in music man perceives the heartbeat of the will of the world.

In music, man feels the echoes of the element that weaves and lives in the innermost core of things, which is so closely related to him. Because feelings are the innermost elements of the soul, akin to the spiritual world, and because in tone the soul finds the element in which it actually moves, man's soul dwells in a world where the bodily mediators of feelings no longer exist but where feelings themselves live on. The archetype of music is in the spiritual, whereas the archetypes for the other arts lie in the physical world itself. When the human being hears music, he has a sense of well-being, because these tones harmonize with what he has experienced in the world of his spiritual home.

II

Through spiritual scientific investigation, we see how the world and all nature surrounding us becomes intelligible. It also becomes increasingly clear to us how the outer facts of our surroundings can have a more-or-less profound significance for the inner being of man. Today we will develop further the theme of why music affects the human soul in such a definite, unique way. In doing this, we will cast light on the very foundations of the soul.

To begin with we must ask how a remarkable hereditary line such as we see in the Bach family, for example, can be explained. Within a period of 250 years, nearly thirty members of this family exhibited marked musical talent. Another case is the Bernoulli family, in which a mathematical gift was inherited in a similar way through several generations, and eight of the family members were mathematicians of some renown. Here are two phenomena that can be understood by heredity, yet they are totally different situations.

To those who have sought to penetrate deeply into the nature of things, music appears to be something quite special. Music has always occupied a special place among the arts. Consider this from Schopenhauer's viewpoint. In his book, *The World as Will and Idea*, he speaks of art as a kind of knowledge that leads more directly to the divine than is possible for intellectual knowledge. This opinion of Schopenhauer's is connected with his world view, which held that everything surrounding us is only a reflection of the human mental image or idea. This reflection arises only because outer things call forth mental images in the human senses, enabling man to relate to the things themselves. Man can know nothing of that which is unable to make an impression on the senses. Schopenhauer speaks physiologically of specific sense impressions. The eye can receive only light impressions; it is insensitive to all other impressions; it can sense only something that is light. Likewise, the ear can sense only tone impressions, and so on. According to Schopenhauer's view, everything observed by man as the world around him reflects itself like a Fata Morgana within him; it is a kind of reflection called forth by the human soul itself.

According to Schopenhauer, there is one possibility of bypassing the mental image. There is one thing perceptible to man for which no outer impression is needed, and this is man himself. All outer things are an eternally changing, eternally shifting Fata Morgana for man. We experience only one thing within ourselves in an immutable manner: ourselves. We experience ourselves in our will, and no detour from outside is required to perceive its effects on us. When we exercise any influence on the outer world, we experience will, we ourselves are this will, and we therefore know what the will is. We know it from our own inner experience, and by analogy we can conclude that this will working within us must exist and be active outside us as well. There must exist forces outside us that are the same as the force active within us as will. These forces Schopenhauer calls "the world will."

Now let us pose the question of how art originates. In line with Schopenhauer's reasoning, the answer would be that art originates through a combination of the Fata Morgana outside us and that within us, through a uniting of both. When an artist, a sculptor, for example, wishes to create an ideal figure, say, of Zeus, and he searches for

11

an archetype, he does not focus on a single human being in order to find the archetype in him; instead, he looks around among many men. He gathers a little from one man, a little from another, and so on. He takes note of everything that represents strength and is noble and outstanding, and from this he forms an archetypal picture of Zeus that corresponds to the thought of Zeus he carries. This is the idea in man, which can be acquired only if the particulars the world offers us are combined within man's mind.

Let us place Schopenhauer's thought alongside one of Goethe's, which finds expression in the words, "In nature, it is the intentions that are significant." We find Schopenhauer and Goethe in complete agreement with one another. Both thinkers believe that there are intentions in nature that she can neither bring completely to expression nor attain in her creations, at least not with the details. The creative artist tries to recognize these intentions in nature; he tries to combine them and represent them in a picture. One now comprehends Goethe, who says that art is a revelation of nature's secret intentions and that the creative artist reveals the continuation of nature. The artist takes nature into himself; he causes it to arise in him again and then lets it go forth from him. It is as if nature were not complete and in man found the possibility of guiding her work to an end. In man, nature finds her completion, her fulfillment, and she rejoices, as it were, in man and his works.

In the human heart lies the capability of thinking things through to the end and of pouring forth what has been the intention of nature. Goethe sees nature as the great, creative artist that cannot completely attain her intentions, presenting us with something of a riddle. The artist, however, solves these riddles; he thinks the intentions of nature through to the end and expresses them in his works.

Schopenhauer says that this holds true of all the arts except music. Music stands on a higher level than all the other arts. Why? Schopenhauer finds the answer, saying that in all the other creative arts, such as sculpture and painting, the mental images must be combined before the hidden intentions of nature are discovered. Music, on the other hand, the melodies and harmonies of tones, is nature's direct expression. The musician hears the pulse of the divine will that flows through the world; he hears how this will expresses itself in tones. The musician thus stands closer to the heart of the world than all other artists; in him lives the faculty of representing the world will. Music is the expression of the will of nature, while all the other arts are expressions of the idea of nature. Since music flows nearer the heart of the world and is a direct expression of its surging and swelling, it also directly affects the human soul. It streams into the soul like the divine in its different forms. Hence, it is understandable that the effects of music on the human soul are so direct, so powerful, so elemental.

Let us turn from the standpoint of significant individuals such as Schopenhauer and Goethe concerning the sublime art of music to the standpoint of spiritual science, allowing it to cast its light on this question. If we do this, we find that what man *is* makes comprehensible why harmonies and melodies affect him. Again, we return to the three states of consciousness that are possible for the human being and to his relationship to the three worlds to which he belongs during any one of these three states of consciousness.

Of these three states of consciousness, there is only one fully known to the ordinary human being, since he is unaware of himself while in either of the other two. From them, he brings no conscious recollection or impression back into his familiar state of consciousness, that is, the one we characterized as waking day-consciousness. The second state of consciousness is familiar to an extent to the ordinary human being. It is dream-filled sleep, which presents simple daily experiences to man in symbols. The third state of consciousness is dreamless sleep, a state of a certain emptiness for the ordinary human being.

Initiation, however, transforms the three states of consciousness. First, man's dream-life changes. It is no longer chaotic, no longer a reproduction of daily experiences often rendered in tangled symbols. Instead, a new world unfolds before man in dream-filled sleep. A world filled with flowing colors and radiant light-beings surrounds him, the astral world. This is no newly created world. It is new only for a person who, until now, had not advanced beyond the lower state of day-consciousness. Actually, this astral world is always present and continuously surrounds the human being. It is a real world, as real as the world surrounding us that appears to us as reality. Once a person has been initiated, has undergone initiation, he becomes acquainted with this wonderful world. He learns to be conscious in it with a consciousness as clear—no even clearer—than his ordinary day-consciousness. He also becomes familiar with his own astral body and learns to live in it consciously. The basic experience in this new world that unfolds before man is one of living and weaving in a world of colors and light. After his initiation, man begins to awaken during his ordinary dream-filled sleep; it is as though he feels himself borne upward on a surging sea of flowing light and colors. This glimmering light and these flowing colors are living beings. This experience of conscious dream-filled sleep then transmits itself into man's entire life in waking day-consciousness,

14

and he learns to see these beings in everyday life as well.

Man attains the third state of consciousness when he is capable of transforming dreamless sleep into a conscious state. This world that man learns to enter shows itself to him at first only partially, but in due time more and more is revealed. Man lives in this world for increasingly longer periods. He is conscious in it and experiences something very significant there.

Man can arrive at perception of the second world, the astral world, only if he undergoes the discipline of so-called "great stillness." He must become still, utterly still, within himself. The great peace must precede the awakening in the astral world. This deep stillness becomes more and more pronounced when man approaches the third state of consciousness, the state in which he begins to have sensations in dreamless sleep. The colors of the astral world become increasingly transparent, and the light becomes ever clearer and at the same time spiritualized. Man has the sensation that he himself lives in this color and this light, as if they do not surround him but rather he himself is color and light. He feels himself astrally within this astral world, and he feels afloat in a great, deep peace. Gradually, this deep stillness begins to resound spiritually, softly at first, then louder and louder. The world of colors and light is permeated with resounding tones. In this third state of consciousness that man now approaches, the colorful world of the astral realm in which he dwelt up to now becomes suffused with sound. This new dimension that opens to man is Devachan, the so-called mental world, and he enters this wondrous world through the portals of the "great stillness." Through the great stillness, the tone of this other world rings out to him. This is how the Devachanic world truly appears.

Many theosophical books contain other descriptions of Devachan, but they are not based on personal experience of the reality of the world. Leadbeater, for example, gives an accurate description of the astral plane and of experiences there, but his description of Devachan is inaccurate. It is merely a construction modeled on the astral plane and is not experienced personally by him. All descriptions that do not describe how a tone rings out from the other side are incorrect and are not based on actual perception. Resounding tone is the particular characteristic of Devachan, at least essentially. Of course, one must not imagine that the Devachanic world does not radiate colors as well. It is penetrated by light emanating from the astral world, for the two worlds are not separated; the astral world penetrates the Devachanic world. The essence of the Devachanic realm, however, lies in tone. That which was light in the great stillness now begins to resound.

On a still higher plane of Devachan, tone becomes something akin to words. All true inspiration originates on this plane, and in this region dwell inspired authors. Here they experience a real permeation with the truths of the higher worlds. This phenomenon is entirely possible.

We must bear in mind that not only the initiate lives in these worlds. The only difference between the ordinary human being and the initiate is that an initiate undergoes these various altered conditions consciously. The states that ordinary man undergoes unconsciously again and again merely change into conscious ones for him. The ordinary human being passes through these three worlds time after time, but he knows nothing about it, because he is conscious neither of himself nor of his experiences there. Nevertheless, he returns with some of the effects that these experiences called forth in him. When he awakens in the morning, not only is he physically rejuvenated by the sleep, but he also brings back art from those worlds. When a painter, for example, goes far beyond the reality of colors in the physical world in his choice of the tones and color harmonies that he paints on his canvas, it is none other than a recollection, albeit an unconscious one, of experiences in the astral world. Where has he seen these tones, these shining colors? Where has he experienced them? They are the after-effects of the astral experiences he has had during the night. Only this flowing ocean of light and colors, of beauty and radiating, glimmering depths, where he has dwelt during sleep, gives him the possibility of using these colors among which he existed. With the dense, earthy colors of our physical world, however, he is unable to reproduce anything close to the ideal that he has experienced and that lives in him. We thus see in painting a shadow-image, a precipitation of the astral world in the physical world, and we see how the effects of the astral realm bear magnificent, marvelous fruits in man.

In great art there are wonderful things that are much more comprehensible to a spiritual scientist, because he discerns their origin. I am thinking, for instance, of two paintings by Leonardo da Vinci that hang in the Louvre in Paris. One portrays Bacchus, the other St. John. Both paintings show the same face; evidently the same model was employed for both. It is not their outward narrative effect, therefore, that makes them totally different from each other. The artistic mysteries of light contained in the paintings are based more purely on their effects of color and light. The painting of Bacchus displays an unusual glistening reddish light that is poured over the body's surface. It speaks of voluptuousness concealed beneath the skin and thus characterizes Bacchus's nature. It is as if the body were imbibing the light and, permeated with its own voluptuous nature, exuded it again. The painting of John, on the other hand, displays a chaste, yellowish hue. It seems as if the color is only playing about the body. The body allows the light only to surround its forms; it does

17

not wish to absorb anything from outside into itself. An utterly unselfish corporeality, fully pure and chaste, addresses the viewer from this painting.

A spiritual scientist understands all this. One must not believe, however, that an artist is always intellectually aware of what is concealed in his work. The precipitations of his astral vision need not penetrate as far as physical consciousness in order to live in his works. Leonardo da Vinci perhaps did not know the occult laws by which he created his paintings—that is not what matters—but he followed them out of his instinctive feeling. We thus see in painting the shadow, the precipitation, of the astral world in our physical realm.

The composer conjures a still higher world; he conjures the Devachanic world into the physical world. The melodies and harmonies that speak to us from the compositions of our great masters are actually faithful copies of the Devachanic world. If we are at all capable of experiencing a foretaste of the spiritual world, this would be found in the melodies and harmonies of music and the effects it has on the human soul.

We return once again to the nature of the human being. We find first of all the physical world, then the etheric body, then the astral body, and finally the "I," of which man first became conscious at the end of the Atlantean age.[3]

When man sleeps, the astral body and the sentient soul release themselves from the lower nature of man. Physical man lies in bed connected with his etheric body. All his other members loosen and dwell in the astral and Devachanic worlds. In these worlds, specifically in the Devachanic world, the soul absorbs into itself the world of tones. When he awakens each morning, man actually has passed through an element of music, an ocean of tones. A musical person is one whose physical nature is such that it follows these impressions, though he need not know this. A sense of musical pleasure is based on nothing other than the right accord between the harmonies brought from beyond and the tones and melodies here. We experience musical pleasure when outer tones correspond with those within.

Regarding the musical element, the cooperation of sentient soul and sentient body is of special significance. One must understand that all consciousness arises through a kind of overcoming of the outer world. What comes to consciousness in man as pleasure or joy signifies victory of the spiritual over merely animated corporeality [Körperlich-Lebendige], the victory of the sentient soul over the sentient body. It is possible for one who returns from sleep with the inner vibrations to intensify these tones and to perceive the victory of the sentient soul over the sentient body, so that the soul feels itself stronger than the body. In the effects of a minor key man can always perceive how the vibrations of the sentient body grow stronger, while in a major key the sentient soul vibrates more intensely and predominates over the sentient body. When the minor third is played, one feels pain in the soul, the predominance of the sentient body, but when the major third resounds, it announces the victory of the soul.

Now we can grasp the basis of the profound significance of music. We understand why music has been elevated throughout the ages to the highest position among the arts by those who know the relationships of the inner life, why even those who do not know these relationships grant music a special place, and why music stirs the deepest strings of our soul, causing them to resound.

Alternating between sleeping and waking, man continuously passes from the physical to the astral and from these worlds to the Devachanic world, a reflection of his overall course of incarnations. When in death he leaves the physical body, he rises through the astral world up into Devachan. There he finds his true home; there he finds his place of rest. This solemn repose is followed by his re-entry into the physical world, and in this way man passes continuously from one world to another.

The human being, however, experiences the elements of the Devachanic world as his own innermost nature, because they are his primeval home. The vibrations flowing through the spiritual world are felt in the innermost depths of his being. In a sense, man experiences the astral and physical as mere sheaths. His primeval home is in Devachan, and the echoes from this homeland, the spiritual world, resound in him in the harmonies and melodies of the physical world. These echoes pervade the lower world with inklings of a glorious and wonderful existence; they churn up man's innermost being and thrill it with vibrations of purest joy and sublime spirituality, something that this world cannot provide. Painting speaks to the astral corporeality, but the world of tone speaks to the innermost being of man. As long as a person is not yet initiated, his homeland, the Devachanic world, is given to him in music. This is why music is held in such high esteem by all who sense such a relationship. Schopenhauer also senses this in a kind of instinctive intuition and expresses it in his philosophical formulations.

Through esoteric knowledge the world, and above all the arts, become comprehensible to us. As it is above so it is below, and as below so above. One who understands this expression in its higher sense learns to recognize increasingly the preciousness in the things of this world, and gradually he experiences as precious recognition the imprints of ever higher and higher worlds. In music, too, he experiences the image of a higher world.

The work of an architect, built in stone to withstand centuries, is something that originates in man's inner being and is then transformed into matter. The same is true of the works of sculptors and painters. These works are present externally and have taken on form.

Musical creations, however, must be generated anew again and again. They flow onward in the surge and swell of their harmonies and melodies, a reflection of the soul, which in its incarnations must always experience itself anew in the onward-flowing stream of time. Just as the human soul is an evolving entity, so its reflection here on earth is a flowing one. The deep effect of music is due to this kinship. Just as the human soul flows downward from its home in Devachan and flows back to it again, so do its shadows, the tones, the harmonies. Hence the intimate effect of music on the soul. Out of music the most primordial kinship speaks to the soul; in the most inwardly deep sense, sounds of home rebound from it. From the soul's primeval home, the spiritual world, the sounds of music are borne across to us and speak comfortingly and encouragingly to us in surging melodies and harmonies.

III

To characterize the theme of today's lecture, we shall begin with an observation already made in the previous lecture. We explained how, in the same way that a man's shadow appears on the wall, a shadow-image of the Devachanic life is given to us on the physical plane in music and generally in the life of tones. We mentioned that twenty-nine more-or-less gifted musicians were born into the Bach family within a period of 250 years and that the musical talent was handed down through the generations just as mathematical talent was handed down in the Bernoulli family. Today we shall illuminate these facts from the esoteric standpoint, and from this standpoint we will receive various answers to important questions about karma. Something that lives as a question in many souls is what the relationship of physical heredity is to what we call an ongoing karma.

In the Bach family, the great-great-grandfather of Johann Sebastian was an individuality who lived on earth some fifteen or sixteen hundred years ago, when the human being was constituted quite differently. In Bach's grandfather another individuality was incarnated. The father is yet again a different individuality, and another incarnates itself in the son. These three individualities have absolutely nothing directly to do with the inheritance of musical talent. Musical talent is transmitted purely within physical heredity. The question of physical heredity is superficially resolved when we realize that man's musical gift depends on a special configuration of the ear. All musical talent is meaningless if a person does not have a musical ear; the ear must be specially adapted for this talent. This purely bodily basis for musical talent is handed down from generation to generation. We thus have a musical son, father, and grandfather, all of whom had musical ears. Just as the physical form of the body—of the nose, for instance—is handed down from one generation to another, so are the structural proportions of the ear.

Let us assume we are dealing with a number of individualities who happen to find themselves in the spiritual world and who bring with them from the previous incarnation the predisposition for music that now wishes to come to expression on the physical plane. What significance would the predisposition have if the individuals could not incarnate in bodies possessing a musical ear? These individualities would have to go through life with this faculty remaining mute and undeveloped. Hence, these individualities naturally feel themselves drawn to a family with a musical ear, with a bodily predisposition that will enable them to realize their potential. The family below on the physical plane exerts a power of attraction on the individuality above in Devachan. Even if the individual's spiritual sojourn perhaps has not been completed and he might have remained another 200 years in Devachan, if a suitable physical body is available on the physical plane, he may incarnate now. Chances are that the individuality will make up the 200 years during his next time in Devachan by remaining there that much longer. Such laws lie at the basis of incarnation, which depends not only on the individuality ready for incarnation but also on the force of attraction being exerted from below. When Germany needed a Bismarck, a suitable individuality had to incarnate, because the circumstances drew him down to the physical plane. The time in the spiritual world thus can be cut short or extended depending on the circumstances on earth that either do or do not press for reincarnation.

To comprehend how the human being is organized, we must look at the nature of man in more detail. Man has a physical, an etheric, and an astral body. He has the physical body in common with all beings one calls inanimate and the etheric body in common with all plants. Then comes the astral body, in itself quite a complicated entity, and finally the "I."

When we examine the astral body closely, we have first the so-called sentient body. This man has in common with the entire animal kingdom, so that all higher animals, just like the human being, possess a physical body, an etheric body, and a sentient body below on the physical plane. Man has an individual soul here on earth, whereas the animal has a group soul. Thus, the animals of a particular species share a common group soul, which can be studied only by ascending to the astral plane. In man's case, however, the soul is here on the physical plane. With the human being, the sentient body is only one part of his astral body. The fourth member of man's organization is the "I," which is active from within.

Let us imagine ourselves back in a distant age, the Lemurian age. Something extremely significant took place during that period. Man's ancestors who existed on earth millions and millions of years ago were completely different from human beings today. On the physical plane of the earth of that time, there was a kind of strangely shaped higher animal, of which nothing remains any longer on the earth today, since it became extinct long ago. The higher animals of today are descendants of those completely differently shaped beings, but they are descendants that have degenerated. Those beings of the ancient past are the ancestors of present-day physical human

24

nature. They possessed only a physical body, an etheric body, and a sentient body. During that age, the "I" gradually united with these beings; it descended from the higher worlds. Animality therefore rose upward toward the human soul, while the soul made its way down from above. Animality developed itself upward, while the soul descended.

As a whirling cloud of dust spirals up from the earth and a rain cloud descends to meet it, so did the animal body and the human soul unite. The sentient body of this animal living below on earth—man's ancestor—had developed itself to the point where it could receive the "I."

This "I" was also composed of various members, namely, the sentient soul, the intellectual soul, and the consciousness soul. Imperceptible to the outer senses, this "I"-body [*Ich-Leib*] descended to meet the upwardly evolving physical body, etheric body, and sentient body.

Had beings possessing a physical body, an etheric body, and a sentient body existed a million years earlier, they would have been able to feel these "I's" hovering above. They would have been forced, however, to say, "A union with such beings is impossible, for the sentient souls hovering above are so delicately spiritual that they are unable to unite themselves with our coarse bodies." Gradually, however, the soul above became coarser and the sentient body below more refined. A kinship came into being between the two, and now the soul descended. Like a sword fits into a scabbard, so the sentient soul fits into the sentient body. We must understand in this sense the words of the Bible: "God breathed into man the breath of life, and he became a living soul." In order to understand these words fully, one must know the various states of matter that exist on earth. First, we have the solid state. The esoteric term for it is the "earth." In using this term, however, the esotericist does not refer to the actual soil of the fields but to its solid condition. All solid components of the physical body—the bones, the muscles, and so forth—are termed "earth." The second state is fluidity; the esoteric term for it is "water." Everything fluid—blood, for instance—is called "water." Third, we have the gaseous state, "air" in esoteric terminology.

The esotericist goes on to consider higher and subtler substances, more delicate states beyond air. In order to understand this better, we must consider, for example, a metal such as lead. In esoteric terminology, lead is "earth." If subjected to intense heat it melts and becomes "water" in the esoteric sense. When it vaporizes it becomes in the esoteric sense "air." Any substance thus can become "air" in its final state. If "air" is more and more diffused, it becomes increasingly delicate and reaches a new state. The esotericist calls it "fire." It is the first state of ether. "Fire" is related to "air" in the same way that "water" is related to solidity. A still more delicate state than "fire" is called "light ether" by the esotericist. Continuing to a still higher state, we come to what esotericists call "chemical ether," which is the force that enables oxygen, for example, to link itself with hydrogen. A still more delicate state than "chemical ether" is "life ether."

We thus have seven different states in esotericism. Life in any substance ultimately can be attributed to the life ether. In esoteric language, what lives in the physical body consists of earth, water, and air. What lives in the etheric body consists of fire, light ether, chemical ether, and life ether. While physical body and etheric body are united, they are at the same time separated. The physical body is permeated by the entire etheric body; similarly the astral body permeates the etheric body. The astral element can descend as far as the state of "fire," but it can no longer mix with "air," "water," and "earth." The physical, on the other hand, can ascend only as far as "fire." Let us make it clear that the physical as vapor or

26

esoteric "air" ascends to "fire"; in the vapor we sense the "fire's" diffusing force. The physical ascends to "fire," the astral descends to "fire," and the etheric body occupies the central position between the two.

In the Lemurian age, a time long before the seven members of man had united, we find beings existing on the physical plane who had not yet brought the physical body to the state of "fire." They were as yet incapable of developing warm blood. Only a physical body capable of developing warm blood links a soul to itself. As soon as those beings had evolved to the level of fire ether, the "I"-soul [*Ich-Seele*] was ready to unite itself with the physical body. All the animals that remained behind as stragglers, such as the amphibians, have blood with variable temperature.

We must keep in mind this point in time from the Lemurian age. It was a moment of the utmost importance, when the being consisting of physical body, etheric body, and sentient body could, through the warm blood, be fructified with a human soul.

Evolution continued from the Lemurian to the Atlantean age. In the Lemurian age, body and soul came in contact with each other only in the element of warmth. At the beginning of the Atlantean age, something new took place. The soul element penetrated more deeply into the physical body, mainly to the level of "air." In the Lemurian age, it had progressed only as far as "fire"; now it penetrated to "air." This is very important for human evolution, since it marks the beginning of the ability to live in the element of air. Just as there were only cold-blooded creatures at the outset of the Lemurian age, so up to now all creatures had been mute and incapable of uttering sound. They had to master the domain of air before they could emit sounds. Now, the first, most elementary beginnings of singing and speaking took place.

The next stage will bring about the soul's descent into

the fluid element. The soul will then be capable of guiding consciously the flow of blood, for example, in the arteries. We will encounter this stage of evolution in the distant future.

One could argue that the cold-blooded insect also "speaks," but in the sense used here, where speaking is the soul resounding outward from within, this is not the case. The sounds made by the insect are of a physical nature. The chirping of the cricket, the whirring of its wings, are outer sounds; it is not the soul that resounds. We are concerned here with the soul's expression in tone.

At the point in time just described, man became capable of pouring forth his soul in sound. He could now emit from within the same element that reached him from outside. Man came to receive tone from outside through the ear and to return it as such to his surroundings. The ear is thus one of the oldest organs and the larynx one of the youngest. The relationship between ear and larynx is different from that between all other organs. The ear itself reverberates; it is like a kind of piano. There are a number of delicate fibers inside the ear, each of which is tuned to a certain tone. The ear does not alter what comes to it from outside, or at least it does so only a little. All the other sense organs, like the eye, for example, alter the impressions received from the environment. All the other senses must develop in the future to the stage of the ear, for in the ear we have a physical organ that stands at the highest level of development.

The ear is also related to a sense that is still older, the sense of spatial orientation that enables one to experience the three dimensions of space. Man is no longer aware of this sense. It is intimately connected with the ear. Deep in the ear's interior we find three remarkable loops, three semi-circular canals that stand perpendicular, one on top of the other. Science does not know what to make of them. When they are injured, however, man's sense of balance is upset. They are the remnants of the sense of space, which is much older than the sense of hearing. Formerly, man perceived space in the same way he perceives tone today. Now the sense of space has become entirely part of him, and he is no longer conscious of it. The sense of space perceives space; the ear perceives tone, which means that which passes from space into time.

Now one will understand how a certain kinship can exist between music and the mathematical sense, which is tied to these three semi-circular canals. The musical family's distinguishing feature is the musical ear. The mathematical family shows a special development of the three semi-circular canals in the ear to which is linked the talent for grasping spatial relationships. These semi-circular canals were particularly developed in the Bernoulli family and passed on from one member to another, just like the musical ear in the Bach family. In order to be able to live fully in their predispositions, individualities descending to incarnation had to seek out the family in which this hereditary trait existed. Such are the intimate relationships between physical heredity and the soul, which seek one another out even after many hundreds and hundreds of years. In this way we see how man's outer nature is connected with his inner being.

IV

In recent discussions,[4] I pointed out that certain human functions appearing in early childhood are transformations of functions that man carries out in pre-earthly existence between death and a new birth. We see how, after birth, the child not fully adapted to the earth's gravity and equilibrium gradually develops to the point at which it becomes adjusted to this equilibrium, how it learns to stand and walk upright. The body's adaptation to the condition of equilibrium of earthly existence is something the human being acquires only after life on earth has begun. We know that the form of man's physical body is the result of a magnificent spiritual activity, which man, together with beings of the higher worlds, undertakes in the period between death and a new birth. What man forms in this way, however—that which becomes the spiritual seed, as it were, for his future physical, earthly organism—does not yet contain the faculty of walking upright. That faculty is incorporated into the human being when he adapts himself after birth to the conditions of equilibrium and gravity of earthly existence.

In pre-earthly existence, orientation does not refer to walking and standing as it does here on earth. There, orientation refers to the relationship man has with angels and archangels and therefore to beings of the higher hierarchies. It is a relationship in which one finds oneself attracted more to one being, less to another; this is the state of equilibrium in the spiritual world. It is lost to a certain extent when man descends to the earth. In the mother's womb, man is neither in the condition of equilibrium of his spiritual life nor yet in that of his earthly life. He has left the former and as yet has not entered the latter.

It is similar in the case of language; the language we speak here on earth is adjusted in every respect to earthly conditions, for this language is an expression of our earthly thoughts. These earthly thoughts contain earthly information and knowledge, and language is adapted to them during earthly existence. In pre-earthly existence, man has a language that does not actually emerge from within, that does not follow the exhalation. Instead, it follows spiritual inhalation, inspiration, something in pre-earthly existence that we can describe as corresponding to inhalation. It is a life within the Word of the universe, the universal language, from which all things are made.

As we descend to the earth, we lose this life within the universal language, and here we acquire the means that serve to express our thoughts, our earthly thoughts, and the human intellect, that is, the intellect among all human beings dwelling on earth. It is the same with the thoughts we have here as with the thinking. Thinking is adapted to earthly conditions. In pre-earthly existence we live within the weaving thoughts of the universe.

If we first focus on the mediating member of man, man's speaking, we can say that an essential part of the earth's culture and civilization lies in speaking. Through speaking, people come together here on earth; speaking is the bridge between two persons. Soul unites with soul. We feel that in speaking we have an essential aspect of life on earth; it is, after all, the earthly reflection of life in the Logos, in the Word of the universe. It is therefore particularly interesting to understand the connection between what man struggles to attain on earth as his language and the metamorphosis of this language found in pre-earthly life. The study of this relationship directs us to the inner organization of man, which stems from the elements of sound and tone. It is especially fitting that at this moment I can add the subject of man's expression through tone and word to the cosmological considerations we have been conducting for weeks. Today we have had the great pleasure of listening to a superb vocal recital here in our Goetheanum. As an expression of inner satisfaction over this gratifying artistic event, let me say something about the connection between man's sound and tone expressions here on earth with man's life in that which corresponds to tone and sound in the spiritual.

If we observe the human organization as it is manifested on earth, it is a reflection of the spiritual through and through. Not only what man bears within himself but everything surrounding him in outer nature is a reflection of the spiritual. When man expresses himself in speech and song, he expresses his whole organization of body, soul, and spirit as a revelation to the outside as well as to himself, to the inside. Man is completely contained, as it were, in what he reveals in sound and tone. How much he is contained within this is revealed when one goes into the details of what man is when he speaks or sings.

Let us begin by considering speech. In the course of humanity's historical evolution, speech has emerged from a primeval song element. The further we go back into prehistoric times, the more speech resembles recitation and finally singing. In very ancient times of man's earthly evolution, his sound and tone expressions were not differentiated into song and speech; instead, they were one. Man's primeval speech may be described as a primeval song. If we examine the present state of speech, which is already far removed from the pure singing element and has instead immersed itself in the prose element and the intellectual element, we have in speech essentially two elements: the elements of consonants and vowels. Everything brought out in speech is composed of the elements of consonants and vowels. The element of consonants is actually based on the delicate sculptural formation of our body [*Körperplastik*]. How we pronounce a B, a P, an L, or an M is based on something having a definite form in our body. In speaking of these forms, one is not always referring only to the apparatus of speech and song; they represent only the highest culmination. When a human being brings forth a tone or sound, his whole organism is actually involved, and what takes place in the song or speech organ is only the final culmination of what goes on within the entire human being. The form of the human organism could be considered in the following way. All consonants contained in a given language are always actually variations of twelve primeval consonants. In Finnish, for example, these twelve primeval consonants are preserved in a nearly pure state. Eleven are retained completely clearly; only the twelfth has become somewhat unclear. [Gap in the transcript.] If the quality of these twelve primeval consonants is correctly comprehended, each one can be represented by a certain form. If they are combined, they in turn represent the complete sculptural form of the human organization. Not speaking symbolically at all, one can say that the human organism is expressed sculpturally through the twelve primeval consonants.

Actually, what is this human organism? Viewed from an artistic standpoint, it is really a musical instrument. Indeed, you can comprehend standard musical instruments, a violin or some other instrument, by looking at them fundamentally from the viewpoint of the consonants, by picturing how they are built, as it were, out of the consonants. When one speaks of consonants, one always feels something that is reminiscent of musical instruments, and

33

the totality and harmony of all consonants represents the sculptural form of the human organism.

The vowel element is the soul playing on this musical instrument. When you observe the consonant and vowel elements of speech, you actually discover a self-expression of the human being in each word and tone. Through the vowels, the soul of man plays on the "consonantism" of the human bodily instrument. If we examine the speech of modern-day civilization and culture, we notice that, to a large extent, the soul makes use of the brain, the head-nerve organism, when it utters vowels. This was not the case to such an extent in earlier times of human evolution. Let me sketch on the blackboard what takes place in the human head-nerve organism.

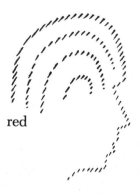

red

The red dotted lines indicate the head-nerve organism. They therefore represent the forces running along the nerve fibers of the head. This is a one-sided view of the whole matter, however. Another activity enters the one generated by the nerve fibers. This new activity is caused by our inhalation of air. Sketching it, we see that the air we inhale passes through the canal of the spinal cord, and the impact of the breathing process unites with the movements taking place along the nerve fibers. The stream of breath (yellow), which pushes upward through the spinal cord to the head, constantly encounters the nerve activity. Nerve activity and breathing activity are not isolated from each other. Instead, an interplay of both takes place in the head. Conditioned by everyday life, man has become prosaic, placing more value on the nerve forces, and he makes more use of his nervous system when he speaks. One could say that he "innergizes" ["*innerviert*," makes inward] the instrument that forms the vowel streams in a consonantal direction. This was not the case in earlier epochs of human evolution. Man lived less in his nervous system; he dwelt more in the breathing system, and for this reason primeval speech was more like song. What man carries out in speech with the help of the "innergizing" of his nervous system he draws back into the stream of breathing when he sings today; he then consciously brings into activity this second stream (sketched in yellow), the stream of breathing. When vowel sounds are added to producing the tone, as in the case of singing, the element of breathing extends into the head and is directly activated from there; it no longer emerges from the breath. It is a return of prosaic speech into the poetic and artistic element of the rhythmic breathing process.

The poet still makes an effort to retain the rhythm of breathing in the way in which he formulates the language of his poems. A person who composes songs takes everything back into breathing, and therefore also into the head-breathing. When man shifts from speaking to singing, he undoes in a certain way what he had to undergo in adapting speech to earthly conditions. Indeed, song is an earthly means of recalling the experiences of pre-earthly existence. We stand much closer to the spiritual world with our rhythmic system than with our thinking system. It is the thinking system that influences speech which has become prosaic.

35

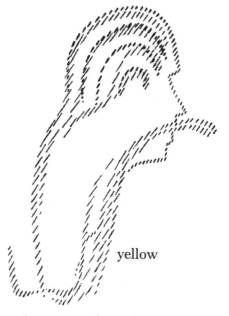

yellow

When producing vowel sounds, we actually push what
lives in the soul toward the body, which serves as the
musical instrument only by adding the consonant element.
Surely you can feel how a soul quality is alive in every
vowel and how you can use the vowel element by itself.
The consonants, on the other hand, tend to long continuously for the vowels. The sculptural instrument of the
body is really dead unless the vowel or soul element touches
it. Many details point to this: take, for instance, the word
"*mir*" ("mine"; pronounced "meer" in high German),
and look at how it is pronounced in some Central Euro-
pean dialects. When I was a little boy, I couldn't imagine
that the word was spelled *m i r*. I always spelled it *m i a*,
because in the *r* is contained the longing for the *a*.

If we see the human organism as the harmony of the

consonants, everywhere we find in it the longing for vowels and therefore the soul element. Why is that? The human organism while here on earth must adapt its sculptural form to earthly conditions. Earthly equilibrium and the configuration of earthly forces determine its shape. Yet, it is really shaped out of the spiritual, and only through spiritual scientific research can one perceive what actually takes place. I shall try to make this clear for you with a diagram. The soul element (red), which expresses itself in vowels, pushes against the element of consonants (yellow). The element of consonants is shaped sculpturally according to earthly conditions.

If one ascends to the spiritual world in the way described in my book, *Knowledge of the Higher Worlds and Its Attainment*,[5] one first acquires imagination, imaginative cognition. Meanwhile, one has lost the consonants, though the vowels still remain. In the imaginative world, one has left one's physical body behind along with the consonants, and one no longer has comprehension for them. If one wishes to describe what is in this higher world adequately in words, one can say that it consists entirely of vowels. Lacking the bodily instrument, one enters a tonal world colored in a variety of ways with vowels. Here, all the earth's consonants are dissolved in vowels. This is why you will find in languages that were closer to the primeval languages that the words for things of the supersensible world were actually vowel-like. The Hebrew word "*Jahve*" for example, did not have the J and the V; it actually consisted only of vowels and was rhythmically half-sung. Using mostly vowels, the words naturally were sung.

In passing from imaginative cognition to cognition through inspiration—where the direct revelations of the spiritual are received—all the consonants that are here on earth become something completely different. The consonants are lost. (See lower yellow lines in sketch below.) In the spiritual perception that can be gained through inspiration, a new element begins to express itself, namely the spiritual counterparts of the consonants. (See upper yellow lines in sketch below.)

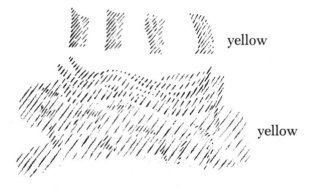

yellow

yellow

These spiritual counterparts of the consonants, however, do not live between the vowels but in them. In languages on earth the consonants and vowels live side by side. The consonants are lost with the ascent into the spiritual world. You live in a singing world of vowels. You yourself actually stop singing; *it* sings. The world itself becomes universal song. The soul-spiritual substance of this vowel element is colored by the spiritual counterparts of the consonants that dwell within the vowels. Here on earth, for example, there is an *a* tone and a c-sharp tone in a certain octave. As soon as one ascends to the spiritual world, there is not just one *a* or one c-sharp of a certain scale; instead, there are untold numbers of them, not just of different pitch but of different inward quality. It is one thing if a being of the hierarchy of angels utters an *a*, another when an archangel or yet another hierarchical being says it. Outwardly it is always the same revelation, but inwardly the revelation is ensouled. We thus can say that here on earth we have our body (sketch on left, white), and a vowel tone (red) pushes against it. Beyond, in the spiritual world, we have the vowel tone (sketch on right, red), and the soul penetrates into it and lives in it so that the tone becomes the soul's body.

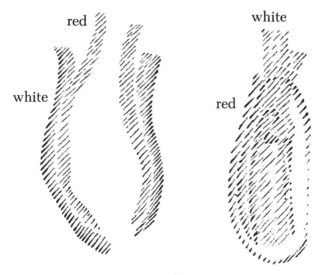

You are now within the universal music, the song of the universe; you are within the creative tone, the creative word. Picture the tone here on earth, even the tone that reveals itself as sound: on earth it lives in the air. The scientific concept, however, that the vibration of the air *is* the tone is a naive concept indeed. Imagine that here is the ground and that someone stands on the ground. Surely the ground is not the person, but it must be there so that the person can stand on it; otherwise he could not be there. You would not want to comprehend man, however, by the ground he stands on. Likewise, tone needs air for support. Just as man stands on the firm ground, so—in a somewhat more complicated way—tone has its ground, its resistance, in the air. Air has no more significance for tone than the ground for the person who stands on it. Tone rushes toward air, and the air makes it possible for tone to "stand." Tone itself, however, is something spiritual. Just as the human being is different from the earthly ground on which he stands, so tone differs from the air on which it rises. Naturally it rises in complicated ways, in manifold ways.

On earth, we can speak and sing only by means of air, and in the air formations of the tone element we have an earthly reflection of a soul-spiritual element. This soul-spiritual element of tone belongs in reality to the super-sensible world, and what lives here in the air is basically the body of tone. It is not surprising, therefore, that one rediscovers tone in the spiritual world, where it is stripped of its earthly garment, the earthly consonants. The vowel element, the spiritual content of tone as such, is taken along when one ascends into the spiritual world, but now it becomes inwardly filled with soul. Instead of being outwardly formed by the element of consonants, the tone is inwardly filled with soul. This runs parallel to one's becoming gradually accustomed to the spiritual world.

Picture how man passes through the portal of death. Soon he leaves the consonants behind, but he experiences the vowels, especially the intonation of the vowels, to a greater degree. He no longer feels that singing is produced by his larynx but that singing is all around him, and he lives in each tone. This is already the case the very first few days after man passes through the portal of death. He dwells, in fact, in a musical element, which is an element of speech at the same time. More and more of the spiritual world reveals itself in this musical element, which is becoming imbued with soul.

As I have explained to you, when man has passed through the portal of death, he passes at the same time from the earthly world into the world of the stars. Though it appears that I am speaking figuratively, this description is a reality. Imagine the earth, surrounding it the planets, and beyond them the fixed stars, which are traditionally pictured, for good reason, as the Zodiac.

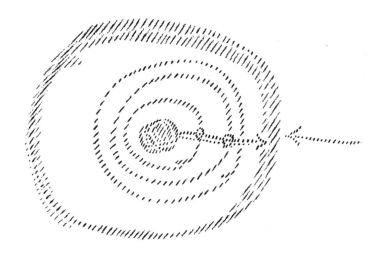

From earth, man views the planets and fixed stars in their reflections; we therefore say that earthly man sees them from the front. The Old Testament expresses this in a different way. When man moves away from the earth after death, he gradually begins to see the planets as well as the fixed stars from behind, as it were. He no longer sees these points or surfaces of light that are seen from the earth; instead, he sees the corresponding spiritual beings. Everywhere he sees a world of spiritual beings. Where he looks back at Saturn, Sun, Moon, Aries, or Taurus, he sees from the other side spiritual beings. Actually, this seeing is also a hearing; and just as one can say that one sees Moon, Venus, Aries, or Taurus from the other side, from behind, so one can say that one hears the beings who have their dwelling places in these heavenly bodies resound into cosmic space.

Picture this whole structure—it sounds as if I speak figuratively, but it is not so, this is a reality; imagine yourself out there in the cosmos: the planetary world further away, the Zodiac with its twelve constellations nearer to you. From all these heavenly bodies it sings to you in speaking, speaks in singing, and your perception is actually a hearing of this speaking-singing, singing-speaking. When you look toward the constellation of Aries you have a soul-consonant impression. Perhaps you behold Saturn behind Aries: now you hear a soul-vowel. In this soul-vowel element, which radiates from Saturn into cosmic space, there lives the soul-spiritual consonant element of Aries or Taurus. You therefore have the planetary sphere that sings in vowels into cosmic space, and you have the fixed stars that ensoul this song of the planetary sphere with consonant elements. Vividly picture the more serene sphere of the fixed stars and behind it the wandering planets. As a wandering planet passes a constellation of fixed stars, not just one tone but a whole world of tones resounds, and another tone world sounds forth as the planet moves from Aries to Taurus. Each planet, however, causes a constellation to resound differently. You have in the fixed stars a wonderful cosmic instrument, and the players of this instrument of the Zodiac and fixed stars are the gods of the planets beyond.

We can truly say that, just as man's walk was shaped for earthly conditions out of cosmic, spiritual orientation, so his speech was shaped for earthly conditions. When man takes speech back into song, he moves closer to the realm of pre-earthly existence, from whence he was born into earthly conditions. It is human destiny that man must adapt himself to earthly conditions with birth. In art, however, man takes a step back, he brings the earthly affairs surrounding him to a halt; once again he approaches the soul-spiritual element from which he emerged out of pre-earthly existence.

We do not understand art if we do not sense in it the longing to experience the spiritual at least in the revelation of beautiful appearance. Our fantasy, which gives rise to the artistic, is basically nothing but the pre-earthly force of clairvoyance. Just as on earth tone lives in the air, so what is actually spiritual in pre-earthly existence lives for the soul element in the earthly reflection of the spiritual. When man speaks, he makes use of his body: the consonant element in him becomes the sculptural form of the body; and the stream of breath, which does not pass into solid, sculptural form, is used by the soul to play on this bodily instrument.

We can, however, direct toward the divine what we are as earthly, speaking human beings in two ways. Take the consonantal human organism; loosen it, as it were, from the solid imprint, which it has received from the earthly forces of gravity or the chemical forces of nutrients; loosen what permeates the human being in a conso-

43

nantal way! We may indeed put it like that. When a human lung is dissected, one finds chemical substances that may be examined chemically. That is not the lung, however. What is the lung? It is a consonant, spoken out of the cosmos, that has taken on form. Put the human heart on the dissecting-table; it consists of cells that can be examined in relation to their chemical substances. That is not the heart, however; the heart is another consonant uttered out of the cosmos. If one pictures in essence the twelve consonants as they are spoken out of the cosmos, one has the human body. This means that if one has the necessary clairvoyant imagination to observe the consonants in their relationships, the complete shape of the human body's sculptural form will arise. If one therefore extracts from the human being the consonants, the art of sculpture arises; if one extracts from the human being the breath, which the soul makes use of in order to play on the instrument in song, if one extracts the vowel element, the art of music, of song, arises.

From the consonant element extracted from the human being, the form arises, which we must shape sculpturally. From the vowel element extracted from the human being arises the musical, the song element, which we must sing. Man, as he stands before us, on earth, is really the result of two cosmic arts. From one direction derives a cosmic art of sculpturing, from the other comes a musical and song-like cosmic art. Two types of spiritual beings fuse their activities. One brings forth and shapes the instrument, the other plays on the instrument.

No wonder that in ancient times, when people were still aware of such things, the greatest artist was called Orpheus. He actually possessed such mastery over the soul element that not only was he able to use the already formed human body as an instrument, but with his tones he could even mold unformed matter into forms that corresponded to the tones.

44

You will understand that when one describes something like this one has to use words somewhat differently from what is customary in today's prosaic age; nevertheless, I did not mean all this figuratively or symbolically but in a very real sense. The matters are indeed as I described them, though the language often needs to be more flexible than it is in today's usage.

The subject of today's lecture was intended by me as a greeting to our two artists[6] who have delighted us with their fine talents. We shall attend tomorrow's concert, my dear friends, with an attitude to which will be added an anthroposophical mood of soul, something that should inform all our endeavors.

V

What we can discuss in these two days will naturally be fragmentary, and I shall address myself chiefly to the needs of teachers. My subject will neither deal with the aesthetics of music nor is it intended for those who wish their enjoyment of art impaired by being told something that is supposed to add to a comprehension of this enjoyment. I would have to speak differently concerning both the aesthetics of music—as conceived from today's standpoint—and the mere enjoyment of it. Now I wish to create a general foundation, and tomorrow I shall go into a few things that can be of significance in preparing such a general foundation in musical instruction. We can go into more detail another time.

It must be pointed out that all the concepts used in other areas of life fail the moment one is obliged to speak about the musical element. It is hardly possible to discuss the musical element in the concepts to which one is accustomed in ordinary life. The reason is simply that the musical element really does not exist in the physical world. It must first be created in the given physical world. This caused people like Goethe to consider the musical element as a kind of ideal of all forms of art. Hence, Goethe said that music is entirely form and substance and requires no other content save that within its own element. This is also why, in the age when intellectualism valiantly struggled for an understanding of music, the strange distinction was made between the content of music and

46

the subject of an art form. Hanslick in particular made this distinction in his book, *The Beautiful in Music*, which emerged out of the above struggle.[7] Naturally, Hanslick ascribes a content to music, though in a one-sided manner, but he denies music a subject. Indeed, music does not have a subject that exists in the outer physical world such as is the case with painting. Even in our age, in which intellectualism wishes to tackle everything, there is a feeling that intellectualism cannot reach the musical element, because it can deal only with something for which there are outer subjects. This explains the strange fact that nowhere in the well-meant instruction of music appreciation does tone physiology (acoustics) have anything to say about the musical element. It is widely admitted that there is a tone physiology only for sounds; there is none for tones. With the means customary today one cannot grasp the element of music. If one does begin to speak about the musical element, it is thus necessary to avoid the ordinary concepts that otherwise we use to grasp our world.

Perhaps the best way to approach what we wish to arrive at in these lectures would be to take present history as our starting point. If we compare our age with former times, we find our age characterized in a specific way in relation to the musical element. One can say that our age occupies a position between two musical feelings [*Empfindungen*]; one such feeling it already has, the other not yet. The feeling that our age has attained, at least to a considerable degree, is the feeling for the interval of the third. In history we can easily trace how the transition from the feeling for the fifth to the third came about in the world of musical feeling. The feeling for the third is something new. The other feeling that will come about but as yet does not exist in our age is the feeling for the octave. A true feeling for the octave actually has not yet

47

developed in humanity. You will experience the difference that exists in comparison to feelings for tone up to the seventh. While the seventh is still felt in relation to the prime, an entirely different experience arises as soon as the octave appears. One cannot actually distinguish it any longer from the prime; it merges with the prime. In any case, the difference that exists for a fifth or a third is absent for an octave. Of course, we do have a feeling for the octave, but this is not yet the feeling that will be developed in time; in the future the feeling for the octave will be something completely different and will one day be able to deepen the musical experience tremendously. Every time the octave appears in a musical composition, man will have a feeling that I can only describe with the words, "I have found my 'I' anew; I am uplifted in my humanity by the feeling for the octave." The particular words I use here are not important; what is important is the feeling that is evoked.

These things can be understood, understood with feeling, only if one becomes clear that the musical experience at first does not have the relationship to the ear that is normally assumed. The musical experience involves the whole human being, and the ear's function in musical experience is completely different from what is normally assumed. Nothing is more incorrect than the simple statement, "I hear the tone or I hear a melody with my ear." That is completely wrong; a tone, a melody, or a harmony actually is experienced with the whole human being. This experience reaches our consciousness through the ear in quite a strange way. As you know, the tones we ordinarily take into consideration have as their medium the air. Even if an instrument other than a wind instrument is used, the element in which tone lives is still the air. What we experience in tone, however, no longer has anything to do with the air. The ear is the organ that first separates

48

the air element from tone before our experience of tone. In experiencing tone as such, we thus actually feel a resonance, a reflection. The ear really hurls the airborne tone back into the inner being of man in such a way that it separates out the air element; then, in that we hear it, the tone lives in the ether element. It is the ear's task—if I may express it in this way—actually to overcome the tone's resounding in the air and to hurl the pure etheric experience of tone back into our inner being. The ear is a reflecting apparatus for the sensation of tone.

Now we must understand the entire tone experience in man more deeply. I must repeat that all concepts come into confusion in encountering the tone experience. We say so lightly that man is a threefold being: nerve-sense man, rhythmic man, and metabolic-limb man. For all other conditions, this is as true as can be. For the tone experience, however, for the musical experience, it is not quite correct. Musical experience does not actually exist in the same sense as sense experience does for the other senses. The sense experience in relation to musical experience is essentially much more introspective than other experiences, because for musical experience the ear is only a reflecting organ; the ear does not actually bring man into connection with the outer world in the same way as does the eye, for example. The eye brings man into connection with all visible forms of the outer world, even artistic forms. The eye is important to a painter, not merely to someone who looks at nature. The ear is important to the musician only in so far as it is in the position of experiencing, without having a relationship to the outer world such as the eye has, for instance. For the musical element, the ear is of importance merely as a reflecting apparatus. We must actually say that regarding the musical experience, we must view the human being first of all as nerve man, because the ear is not important as a direct sense organ but instead as transmitter to man's inner being. The ear is not a link to the outer world—the perception of instrumental music is a quite complicated process about which we shall speak later—and is of no immediate importance as a sense organ but only as a reflecting organ.

Continuing further, what is important in the musical experience is that which is related to man's limb system, through which the element of music can pass into that of dance. Man's metabolic system, however, is not as important here as it is otherwise. In speaking of the musical experience, therefore, we discover a shifting of man's three-fold organization and find that we must say: nerve man, rhythmic man, limb man (not metabolic-limb man). Sense perceptions are ruled out as accompanying factors. They are there because man is a sense being, and his ear also has significance as a sense organ, but not the significance we must ascribe to it in other conditions of the world. The metabolism is also an accompanying factor and does not exist in the same way as elsewhere. Metabolic phenomena appear, but they have no significance. Everything that lives in the limbs as potential for movement, however, has tremendous significance for the musical experience, since dance movements are linked with the musical experience. A great portion of the musical experience consists of one's having to restrain oneself from making movements along with the music. This points out to us that the musical experience is really an experience of the whole human being.

Why is it that man today has an experience of the third? Why is he only on the way to acquiring an experience of the octave? The reason is that in human evolution all musical experience first leads back to the ancient Atlantean time—unless we wish to go back further, which serves no purpose here. The experience of the seventh was the essential musical experience of the ancient Atlantean age. If you could go back into the Atlantean age, you would find that the music of that time, which had little similarity to today's music, was arranged according to continuing sevenths; even the fifth was unknown. This musical experience, which was based on an experience of the seventh through the full range of octaves, always consisted of man feeling completely transported [*entrückt*]. He felt free of his earthbound existence and transported into another world in this experience of the seventh. At that time he could just as well have said, "I experience music," as, "I feel myself in the spiritual world." This was the predominant experience of the seventh. Up into the post-Atlantean age, this continued to play a great role, until it began to have an unpleasant effect. As the human being wished to incarnate more deeply into his physical body and take possession of it, the experience of the seventh became faintly painful. Man began to find the experience of the fifth more pleasant, and for a long time a scale composed according to our standards would have consisted of d, e, g, a, b, and again d and e. There was no f and no c. For the early post-Atlantean epochs, the feeling for f and c is missing; instead, the fifths throughout the tonal range of different octaves were experienced.

In the course of time, the fifths began to be the pleasurable experience. All musical forms, however, in which the third and what we call c today are excluded, were permeated with a measure of this transporting quality. Such music made a person feel as if he were carried into a different element. In the music of the fifths [*Quintenmusik*], a human being felt lifted out of himself. The transition to the experience of the third actually can be traced back into the fourth post-Atlantean epoch, in which experiences of the fifth still predominated. (To this day, experiences of the fifth are contained in native

51

Chinese music.) This transition to the experience of the third signifies at the same time that man feels music in relation to his own physical organization. For the first time, man feels that he is an earthly being when he plays music. Formerly, when he experienced fifths, he would have been inclined to say, "The angel in my being is beginning to play music. The muse in me speaks." "I sing" was not the appropriate expression. It became possible to say this only when the experience of the third emerged, making the whole musical feeling an inward experience; the human being then felt that he himself was singing.

In the age when the fifths predominated, it was impossible to color music in a subjective direction. Subjectivity only came into play in that the subjective felt transported, lifted into objectivity. Not until man could experience the third did the subjective element feel that it rested within itself. Man began to relate the feeling for his destiny and ordinary life to the musical element.

Something now began to have meaning that would have had none in the ages of the experience of the fifth, namely major and minor keys. One could not even have spoken then of a major key. Major and minor keys, this strange bond between music and human subjectivity, the actual inner life of feeling—in so far as this life of feeling is bound to the earthly corporeality—come into being only in the course of the fourth post-Atlantean epoch and are related to the experience of the third. The difference between major and minor keys appears; the subjective soul element relates itself to the musical element. Man can color the musical element in various ways. He is in himself, then outside himself; his soul swings back and forth between self-awareness and self-surrender. Only now is the musical element drawn into the human being in a corresponding way. One thus can say that the experience of the third begins during the fourth post-Atlantean epoch and with it the ability to express major and minor moods in music. Basically, we ourselves are still involved in this process. Only an understanding of the whole human being—one that must reach beyond ordinary concepts—can illustrate how we are involved in this process.

One naturally gets into the habit of speaking in general concepts even in anthroposophy. One thus says that man consists of physical body, etheric body, astral body, and "I." One has to put it like that to begin with in order to describe the human being in stages, but actually the matter is more complicated than one thinks. When we look at the embryonic development of earthly man, we find that, preceding his descent from the spiritual world to the physical world, the human "I" descends spiritually to the astral and etheric. In penetrating the astral and etheric, the "I" is then able to take hold of the physical embryo, giving rise to the forces of growth and so on. Though physical forces take hold of the human embryo, they in turn have been affected by the descent of the "I" through the astral and etheric into the physical. In the fully developed human being living in the physical world, the "I" works spiritually, through the eye, for example, directly upon the physical, at first bypassing the astral and etheric. Later, from within the human organism, the "I" connects itself again with the astral and etheric. We bring into ourselves the etheric and astral only from within out. We thus can say that the "I" lives in us in a twofold way. First, inasmuch as we have become human beings on earth, the "I" lives in us by having descended into the physical world in the first place. The "I" then builds up from the physical with the inclusion of the astral and etheric. Secondly, when we are adults, the "I" dwells in us by virtue of gaining influence over us through the senses or by taking hold of our astral nature. There it gains influence over our breath to the exclusion of the actual "I"-sphere of the head, where the physical body becomes the organ of the "I." Only in the movements of our limbs—if we move our limbs today—do we still have in us the same activity of nature or the world that we had within us as embryos. Everything else is added. The same activity that worked in you when you were an embryo is active today when you walk or dance. All other activities, especially the activity of the head, came about later as the downward streams of development were eliminated.

Now the musical experience actually penetrates the whole human being. The cause for this is the spiritual element that descended the farthest and took hold of the as-yet formless earthly being in, I would like to say, an other-than-human manner. It then laid the foundation for embryonic development and today expresses itself in our movements and gestures. This element that dwells thus in man is at the same time the basis of the lower tones of an octave, namely c, c-sharp, d, and d-sharp. Now, disorder comes in—as you can see on the piano—because the matter reaches the etheric. Everything in man's limb system—in other words, his most physical component—is engaged with the lowest tones of each and every octave. Beginning with e, the vibrating of the etheric body plays an essential role. This continues to f, f-sharp, and g. Beyond this point, the vibrations of the astral body enter in. Now we reach a climactic stage. Beginning with c and c-sharp, when we reach the seventh we come to a region where we actually must stand still. The experience comes to a halt, and we need a completely new element.

By beginning from the first tone of the octave, we have begun from the inner "I," the physical, living, inner "I"—if I may express it in this way—and we have ascended through the etheric and astral bodies to the seventh. We must now pass over to the directly experienced "I," in

54

that we arrive at the next higher octave. We must say, as it were: man actually lives in us in all seven tones, but we do not know it. He pushes against us in c and c-sharp. Pushing upward from there, in f and f-sharp, he shakes up our etheric and astral bodies. The etheric body vibrates and pushes up to the astral body—the origin of the vibration being below in the etheric body—and we arrive at the astral experience in the tones up to the seventh. We do not know it fully, however; we know it only through feeling. Finally, the feeling for the octave brings us to find our own self on a higher level. The third guides us to our inner being; the octave leads us to have, to feel, our own self once more. You must take all these concepts that I use only as substitutes and in each case resort to feelings. Then you will be able to see how the musical experience really strives to lead man back to what he lost in primeval times. In primeval times, when the experience of the seventh existed—and therefore, in fact, the experience of the entire scale—man felt that he was a unified being standing on earth; at that time when he heard the seventh, he also experienced himself outside his body. He therefore felt himself in the world. Music was for him the possibility of feeling himself in the world. The human being could receive religious instruction by being taught the music of that time. He could readily understand that through music man is not only an earthly being but also a transported being. In the course of time, this experience increasingly intensified. The experience of the fifth arose, and during this time man still felt united with what lived in his breath. He said to himself—though he did not say it, he felt it; in order to express it, we must word it like that—"I breathe in, I breath out. During a nightmare I am especially aware of the experience of breath due to the change in my breathing. The musical element, however, does not live in me at all; it lives in inhalation and exhalation." Man felt always as if he were leaving and returning to himself in the musical experience. The fifth comprised both inhalation and exhalation; the seventh comprised only exhalation. The third enabled man to experience the continuation of the breathing process within. Based on all this, you find a specific explanation for the advancement from the pure singing-with-accompaniment that existed in ancient times of human evolution to independent singing. Originally, singing was always produced along with some outer tone, an outer tone structure [*Tongebilde*]. Emancipated singing actually came about later; emancipated instrumental music is connected with that. One can now say that in the musical experience man experienced himself as being at one with the world. He experienced himself neither within nor outside himself. He would have been incapable of hearing an instrument alone; in the very earliest time he could not have heard one isolated tone. It would have appeared to him like a lone ghost wandering around. He could only experience a tone composed of outer, objective elements and inner, subjective ones. Hence, the musical experience was divided into these two, the objective and the subjective.

This whole experience naturally penetrates today into everything musical. On the one hand, music occupies a special position in the world, because, as yet, man cannot find the link to the world in the musical experience. This link to the world will be discovered one day when the experience of the octave comes into being in the manner previously outlined. Then, the musical experience will become for man proof of the existence of God, because he will experience the "I" twice: once as physical, inner "I," the second time as spiritual, outer "I." When octaves are employed in the same manner as sevenths, fifths, and thirds—today's use of octaves does not approach this yet —it will become a new form of proving the existence of

56

God. That is what the experience of the octave will be. People will say to themselves, "When I first experience my 'I' as it is on earth, in the prime, and then experience it a second time the way it is in spirit, then this is inner proof of God's existence." This is a different kind of proof, however, from that of the ancient Atlantean, which he gained through his experience of the seventh. Then, all music was evidence of God's existence, but it was in no way proof of man's existence. The great spirit took hold of the human being and filled him inwardly the moment he participated in music. The great progress made by humanity in the musical element is that the human being is not just possessed by God but takes hold of his own self as well, that man feels the musical scale as himself, but himself as existing in both worlds. You can imagine the tremendous profundity of which the musical element will be capable in the future. Not only will it offer man what he can experience in our ordinary musical compositions today, which have come a long way indeed, but man will be able to experience how, while listening to a musical composition, he becomes a totally different person. He will feel changed, and yet again he will feel returned to himself. The further cultivation of the musical element consists of this feeling of a widely diverse human potential. We thus can say that f has already joined the five old tones, d, e, g, a, and b, to the greatest possible extent, but not yet the actual c. This must still be explored in its entire significance for human feeling.

All this is extraordinarily important when one is faced with the task of guiding the evolution of the human being regarding the musical element. You see, up to about the age of nine, the child does not yet possess a proper grasp of major and minor moods, though one can approach the child with them. When entering school, the child can experience major and minor moods in preparation for what is to come later, but the child has neither one nor the other. Though it is not readily admitted, the child essentially dwells in moods of fifths. Naturally, one can resort in school to examples already containing thirds, but if one really wishes to reach the child, musical appreciation must be based on the appreciation of fifths; this is what is important. One does the child a great kindness if one confronts it with major and minor musical moods as well as an appreciation for the whole third-complex sometime after the age of nine, when the child asks important questions of us. One of the most significant questions concerns the urge for living together with the major and minor third. This is something that appears between ages nine and ten and that should be specifically cultivated. As far as is possible within present-day limits of music, it is also necessary to try to promote appreciation of the octave at around age twelve. What must be offered the child in the way of music thus will be adapted once again to the various ages.

It is tremendously important to be clear that music fundamentally lives only inwardly in man, namely, in the etheric body; regarding the lowest tones of the scale, the physical body is naturally taken along too. The physical body, however, must push upward into the etheric body, which in turn pushes upon the astral body. The "I," finally, can barely be touched.

While we always dwell within our brains with our crude and clumsy concepts regarding the rest of the world, we leave the musical element the instant we develop concepts about it. This is because the unfolding of concepts takes place on a level above that of the musical realm. We must leave music behind when we think, because tone begins to develop shades within itself—prosaic science would say that it exhibits a particular number of vibrations—and is no longer experienced as tone.

When tone begins to develop shades within itself, the concept arises that becomes objectified in sound [*im laut*]. In the sound of speech, the concept really cancels out the tone, in so far as tone is sound, though not in so far as tone harmonizes with the sound, of course. Then, the actual musical experience reaches down only to the etheric body, and there it struggles. Certainly the physical pushes upward into the lower tones. If, however, we were to go all the way down into the physical, the metabolism would be included in the musical experience, which would then cease to be a pure musical experience. In fact, this is attained in the contra-tones so as to make the musical experience somewhat more piquant, as it were. Music is driven slightly out of its own element in the contra-tones.[8] The actual musical experience that takes its course completely within—neither in the "I" nor in the physical body but in etheric and astral man—the inwardly complete musical experience reaches only as far as the etheric body, i.e., down to the tones of the great octave.[9] The contra-tones below only serve the purpose of allowing the outer world to beat, as it were, upon the musical element. The contra-tones appear when man strikes outward with the musical element and the outer world rejects it. This is where the musical element leaves the soul element and enters that of matter. When we descend to the contra-tones, our soul reaches down into the element of matter, and we experience how matter strives to become musically ensouled. This is what the position of contra-tones in music basically signifies.

All this leads us to say that only a truly irrational understanding—an understanding of the human being beyond the rational—will permit us to grasp the musical element in a feeling way and to acquaint the human being with it.

We shall continue in more detail tomorrow.

VI

Though they are quite fragmentary and incomplete and must be elaborated further at the next opportunity, I wish to emphasize again that yesterday's lecture and today's are intended to give teachers in school what they need as background for their instruction.

Yesterday, I spoke on the one hand of the role that the interval of the fifth plays in musical experience and on the other hand of the roles played by the third and the seventh. You have been able to gather from this description that music progressing in fifths is still connected with a musical experience in which the human being is actually brought out of himself; with the feeling for the fifth, man actually feels transported. This becomes more obvious if we take the scales through the range of seven octaves—from the contra-tones up to the tones above c—and consider that it is possible for the fifth to occur twelve times within these seven scales. In the sequence of the seven musical scales, we discover hidden, as it were, an additional twelve-part scale with the interval of the fifth.

What does this really mean in relation to the whole musical experience? It means that within the experience of the fifth man with his "I" is in motion outside his physical organization. He paces the seven scales in twelve steps, as it were. He is therefore in motion outside his physical organization through the experience of the fifth.

Returning to the experience of the third—in both the major and minor third—we arrive at an inner motion of

60

the human being. The "I" is, so to speak, within the confines of the human organism; man experiences the interval of the third inwardly. In the transition from a third to a fifth—though there is much in between with which we are not concerned here—man in fact experiences the transition from inner to outer experience. One therefore can say that in the case of the experience of the third the mood is one of consolidation of the inner being, of man's becoming aware of the human being within himself. The experience of the fifth brings awareness of man within the divine world order. The experience of the fifth is, as it were, an expansion into the vast universe, while the experience of the third is a return of the human being into the structure of his own organization. In between lies the experience of the fourth.

The experience of the fourth is perhaps one of the most interesting for one who wishes to penetrate the secrets of the musical element. This is not because the experience of the fourth in itself is the most interesting but because it arises at the dividing line between the experience of the fifth of the outer world and the experience of the third in man's inner being. The experience of the fouth lies right at the border, as it were, of the human organism. The human being, however, senses not the outer world but the spiritual world in the fourth. He beholds himself from outside, as it were (to borrow an expression referring to vision for an experience that has to do with hearing). Though man is not conscious of it, the sensation he experiences with the fourth is based on feeling that man himself is among the gods. While he has forgotten his own self in the experience of the fifth in order to be among the gods, in the experience of the fourth he need not forget his own being in order to be among the gods. With the experience of the fourth, man moves about, as it were, in the divine world; he stands precisely at the border of his humanness, retaining it, yet viewing it from the other side.

The experience of the fifth as spiritual experience was the first to be lost to humanity. Modern man does not have the experience of the fifth that still existed, let us say, four to five hundred years before our era. At that time the human being truly felt in the experience of the fifth, "I stand within the spiritual world." He required no instrument in order to produce outwardly the interval of a fifth. Because he still possessed imaginative consciousness, he felt that the fifth, which he himself had produced, took its course in the divine realm. Man still had imaginations, still had imaginations in the musical element. There was still an objectivity, a musical objectivity, in the experience of the fifth. Man lost this earlier than the objective experience of the fourth. The experience of the fourth, much later on, was such that during this experience man believed that he lived and wove in something etheric. With the experience of the fourth he felt—if I may say so—the holy wind that had placed him into the physical world. Based on what they said, it is possible that Ambrose and Augustine still felt this. Then this experience of the fourth was also lost. One required an outer instrument in order to be objectively certain of the fourth.

We thus have pointed out at the same time what the musical experience was like in very ancient ages of human evolution. Man did not yet know the third; he descended only to the fourth. He did not distinguish between, "I sing," and "There is singing." These two were one for him. He was outside himself when he sang, and at the same time he had an outer instrument. He had an impression, an imagination, as it were, of a wind instrument, or of a string instrument. Musical instruments appeared to man at first as imaginations. Musical instruments were not invented through experimentation; with the exception of the piano they have been derived from the spiritual world.

With this, we have described the origin of song as well. It is hard today to give an idea of what song itself was like in the age when the experience of the fifth was still pure. Song was indeed something akin to an expression of the word. One sang, but this was at the same time a speaking of the spiritual world. One was conscious that if one spoke of cherries and grapes one used earthly words; if one spoke of the gods, one had to sing.

Then came the time when man no longer had imaginations. He still retained the remnants of imaginations, however, though one does not recognize them as such today—they are the words of language. The spiritual element incarnated into the tones of song, which in turn incarnated into the elements of words. This was a step into the physical world. The inner emancipation of the song element into arias and the like took place after that; this was a later development.

If we return to the primeval song of humanity, we find that it was a speaking of the gods and of the proceedings of the gods. As I mentioned earlier, the fact of the twelve fifths in the seven scales is evidence that the possibility of motion outside the human realm existed in music in the interval of the fifth. Only with the fourth does man really approach himself with the musical element.

Yesterday, someone said quite rightly that man senses an emptiness in the interval of the fifth. Naturally, he must experience something empty in the fifth, since he no longer has imaginations, and the fifth corresponds to an imagination while the third corresponds to a perception within man's being. Today, therefore, man feels an emptiness in the fifth and must fill it with the substantiality of

63

the instrument. This is the transition of the musical element from the more spiritual age to the later materialistic age.

For earlier ages, the relationship of musical man to his instrument must be pictured as the greatest possible unity. A Greek actor even felt the need of amplifying his voice with an instrument. The process of drawing the musical experience inward came later. Formerly, man felt that in relation to music he carried a certain circle of tones within himself that reached downward, excluding the realm of tones below the contra-c. Upward, it did not reach the tones beyond c but was a closed circle. Man then had the consciousness, "I have been given a narrow circle of the musical element. Out there in the cosmos the musical element continues in both directions. I need the instruments in order to reach this cosmic musical element."

Now we must take the other aspects of music into consideration if we wish to become acquainted with this whole matter. The center of music today is harmony. I am referring to the sum total of music, not song or instrumental music. The element of harmony takes hold directly of human feeling. What is expressed in harmonies is experienced by human feeling. Now, feeling is actually the center of the total human experience. On one side, feeling passes over into willing; on the other side, feeling passes into thinking [*Vorstellen*].[10] In looking at the human being, we can say that we have feeling in the middle; on the one hand we have the feeling that passes into thinking, on the other hand we have the feeling that passes into willing. Harmony directly addresses itself to feeling and is experienced in it. The whole emotional nature of man, however, is actually twofold. We have a feeling that is more inclined to thinking—when we feel our thoughts, for instance—and we have a feeling more inclined to willing. When we engage in an action, we feel whether it pleases

64

or displeases us; in the same way, we feel pleasure or displeasure with an idea. Feeling is actually divided into these two realms.

The peculiar thing about the musical element is that neither must it penetrate completely into thinking—because it would cease to be something musical the moment it was taken hold of by the brain's conceptual faculty—nor should it sink down completely into the sphere of willing. We cannot imagine, for example, that the musical element itself could become a direct will impulse without being an abstract sign. When you hear the ringing of the dinner bell, you will go because it announces that it is time to go to dinner, but you will not take the bell's musical element as the impulse for the will. This illustrates that music should not reach into the realm of willing any more than into that of thinking. In both directions it must be contained. The musical experiences must take place within the realm situated between thinking and willing. It must unfold in that part of the human being that does not belong at all to ordinary day-consciousness but that has something to do with that which comes down from spiritual worlds, incarnates, and then passes again through death. It is present in the subconscious, however. For this reason, music has no direct equivalent in outer nature. In adapting himself to the earth, man finds his way into what can be grasped conceptually and what he wills to do. Music, however, does not extend this far into thinking and willing; yet, the element of harmony has a tendency to stream, as it were, toward thinking. It must not penetrate thinking, but it streams toward it. This streaming into the region of our spirit, where we otherwise think [*vorstellen*], is brought about by the harmony out of the melody.

The element of melody guides the musical element from the realm of feeling up to that of thinking. You do not find what is contained in thinking in the thematic melody, but the theme does contain the element that reaches up into the same realm where mental images are otherwise formed. Melody contains something akin to mental images, but it is not a mental image; it clearly takes its course in the life of feeling. It tends upward, however, so that the feeling is experienced in the human head. The significance of the element of melody in human nature is that it makes the head of the human being accessible to feelings. Otherwise, the head is only open to the concept. Through melody the head becomes open to feeling, to actual feeling. It is as if you brought the heart into the head through melody. In the melody you become free, as you normally are in thinking; feeling becomes serene and purified. All outer aspects are eliminated from it, but at the same time it remains feeling through and through.

Just as harmony can tend upward toward thinking, so it can tend downward toward willing. It must not penetrate the realm of willing, however; it must restrain itself, as it were, and this is accomplished through the rhythm. Melody thus carries harmony upward; rhythm carries harmony in the direction of willing. This is restricted willing, a measured will that runs its course in time; it does not proceed outward but remains bound to man himself. It is genuine feeling that extends into the realm of willing.

Now it becomes understandable that when a child first enters school, it comprehends melodies more readily than harmonies. Of course, one must not take this pedantically; pedantry must never play a role in the artistic. It goes without saying that one can introduce the child to all sorts of things. Just as the child should comprehend only fifths during the first years of school—at most also fourths, but not thirds; it begins to grasp thirds inwardly only from age nine onward—one can also say that the child easily understands the element of melody, but it begins to understand the element of harmony only when it reaches the age of nine or ten. Naturally, the child already understands the tone, but the actual element of harmony can be cultivated in the child only after the above age has been reached. The rhythmic element, on the other hand, assumes the greatest variety of forms. The child will comprehend a certain inner rhythm while it is still very young. Aside from this instinctively experienced rhythm, however, the child should not be troubled until after it is nine years old with the rhythm that is experienced, for example, in the elements of instrumental music. Only then should the child's attention be called to these things. In the sphere of music, too, the age levels can indicate what needs to be done. These age levels are approximately the same as those found elsewhere in Waldorf education.

Taking a closer look at rhythm, we see that since the rhythmic element is related to the nature of will—man must inwardly activate his will when he wishes to experience music—it is the rhythmic element that kindles music in the first place. Regardless of man's relationship to rhythm, all rhythm is based on the mysterious connection between pulse and breath, the ratio of eighteen breaths per minute to an average of seventy-two pulse beats per minute. This ratio of 1:4 naturally can be modified in any number of ways; it can also be individualized. Each person has his own experience regarding rhythm; since these experiences are approximately the same, however, people understand each other in reference to rhythm. All rhythmic experience bases itself on the mysterious relationship between breathing and the heartbeat, the circulation of the blood. One thus can say that while the melody is carried from the heart to the head on the stream of breath—and therefore in an outer slackening and inner creation of quality—the rhythm is carried on the waves of the blood circulation from the heart to the limbs, and in the limbs it is arrested as willing. From this you can see how the musical element really pervades the whole human being.

Picture the whole human being who experiences the musical element as a human spirit: the ability to experience the element of melody gives you the head of this spirit. The ability to experience the element of harmony gives you the chest, the central organ of the spirit; and the ability to experience rhythm gives you the limbs of the spirit. What have I described for you here? I have described the human etheric body. If only you depict the whole musical experience, and if you do this correctly, you actually have before you the human etheric body. It is just that instead of "head" we say, "melody"; instead of "rhythmic man"—because it is lifted upward—we say, "harmony"; and instead of "limb man"—we cannot say here, "metabolic man"—we say, "rhythm." We have the entire human being etherically before us. The musical experience is nothing else than this. The human being really experiences himself as etheric body in the experience of the fourth, but a kind of summation forms within him. The experience of the fourth contains a touch of melody, a touch of harmony, a touch of rhythm, but all interwoven in such a way that they are no longer distinguishable. The entire human being is experienced spiritually at the threshold in the experience of the fourth: one experiences the etheric human being.

If today's music were not a part of the materialistic age, if all that man experiences today did not contaminate the musical element, then, based on what man possesses today in the musical element—which in itself has attained world-historical heights—he could not but be an anthroposophist. If you wish to experience the musical element consciously, you cannot but experience it anthroposophically.

If you take these things as they are, you can ponder, for example, over the following point: everywhere in ancient traditions concerning spiritual life, mention is made of man's sevenfold nature. The theosophical movement also adopted this view of the sevenfold nature of the human being. When I wrote my *Theosophy*,[11] I had to speak of a ninefold nature, further dividing the three individual members. I arrived at the sevenfold from a ninefold organization.

9 (spirit man)
8 (life spirit)
7 (spirit self)

6 (consciousness soul)
5 (intellectual soul)
3 (astral or sentient body) 4 (sentient soul)
2 (etheric body)
1 (physical body)

Since three and four overlap, as do six and seven, I, too, arrived at the sevenfold human being in *Theosophy*. This book, however, never could have been written in the age dominated by the experience of the fifth. The reason is that in that age all spiritual experience resulted from the awareness that the number of planets was contained in the seven scales, and the number of signs in the Zodiac was contained in the twelve fifths within the seven scales. The great mystery of man was revealed in the circle of fifths, and in that period you could not write about theosophy in any way but by arriving at the sevenfold human being. My *Theosophy* was written in an age during which predominantly the third is experienced by human beings, in other words, in the age of introversion. One must seek the spiritual in a similar way, descending from the interval of the fifth by division to the interval of the third. I therefore also had to divide the individual members of man. You can say that those other books that speak of the sevenfold human being stem from the tradition of the age of fifths, from the tradition of the circle of fifths. My *Theosophy* is from the age in which the third plays the dominant musical role and in which, because of this, the complication arises that the more inward element tends toward the minor side, the more outward element toward the major side. This causes the indistinct overlapping between the sentient body and sentient soul. The sentient soul relates to the minor third, the sentient body to the major third. The facts of human evolution are expressed in musical development more clearly than anywhere else. As I already told you yesterday, however, one must forego concepts; abstract conceptualizing will get you nowhere here.

When it comes to acoustics, or tone physiology, there is nothing to be gained. Acoustics has no significance, except for physics. A tone physiology that would have significance for music itself does not exist. If one wishes to comprehend the musical element, one must enter into the spiritual.

You see how the interval of the fourth is situated between the fifth and the third. Man feels transported in the fifth; in the third he feels himself within himself; in the fourth he is on the border between himself and the world. Yesterday I told you that the seventh was the dominant interval for the Atlanteans. They had only intervals of the seventh, though they did not have the same feeling as we have today. When they made music they were transported completely beyond themselves; they were within the great, all-pervading spirituality of the universe in an absolute motion. They were being moved. This motion was still contained in the experience of the fifth as well. Again, the sixth is in between. From this we realize that man experiences these three steps, the seventh, the sixth, and the fifth, in a transported condition; he enters into his own being in the fourth; he dwells within himself in the third. Only in the future will man experience the octave's full musical significance. A bold experience of the second has not yet been attained by him today; these are matters that lie in the future. When man's inner life intensifies, he will experience the second, and finally he will be sensitive to the single tone. I do not know whether some of you will recall that I once said during a question-and-answer session in Dornach that the single tone will be experienced as something that is musically differentiated, that already musical differentiation resides within the single tone.

If you focus on what is said here, you will grasp better the forms that appear in our tone eurythmy. You will also grasp something else. You will, for example, grasp the reason that out of instinct the feeling will arise to interpret the lower segments of the octave—the prime, second, and third—by backward movements and in the case of the upper tones—the fifth, sixth, and seventh—by forward movements.

These are more or less the forms that can be used as stereotypical forms, as typical forms. In the case of the forms that have been developed for individual musical compositions, you will be able to sense that these forms express the experience of the fourth or the fifth.

71

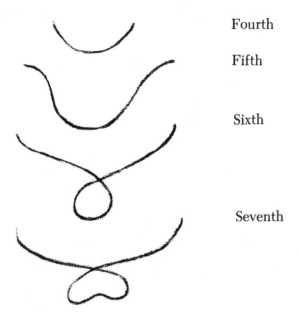

Fourth

Fifth

Sixth

Seventh

In eurythmy it is necessary that this part here—the descent of harmony through rhythm into willing—finds emphatic expression in form. The individual intervals thus are contained in the forms as such, executed by the eurythmist. Then, however, that which passes from the intervals into rhythm must be experienced fully by the performer in these forms; and quite by itself the instinct will arise to make as small a movement as possible without standing still in the case of the fourth. You see, the fourth is in fact a real perceiving, but a perceiving from the other side. It would be as if the eye, in perceiving itself, would have to look back upon itself; this, then, is the experience of the fourth gained from the soul.

The interval of the fifth is a real experience of imagination. He who can experience fifths correctly is actually in a position to know on the subjective level what imagination is like. One who experiences sixths knows what inspiration is. Finally, one who fully experiences sevenths—if he survives this experience—knows what intuition is. What I mean is that in the experience of the seventh the form of the soul's composition is the same as clairvoyantly with intuition. The form of the soul's composition during the experience of the sixth is that of inspiration with clairvoyance. The experience of the fifth is a real imaginative experience. The same composition of soul need only be filled with vision. Such a composition of soul is definitely present in the case of music.

This is why you hear everywhere that in the older mystery schools and remaining mystery traditions clairvoyant cognition is also called a musical cognition, a spiritual-musical cognition. Though people today no longer know why, the mysteries refer to the existence of two kinds of cognition, ordinary bodily, intellectual cognition and spiritual cognition, which is in fact a musical cognition, a cognition living in the musical element. It would not actually be so difficult to popularize the understanding of the threefold human being if only people today were conscious of their musical experiences. Certainly to some extent people do have sensitivity for music, but, as human beings, they are not really within the experience of the musical element. They actually stand alongside it. The experience of the musical element is as yet quite limited. If it were really to become alive in man, he would feel: my etheric head is in the element of melody, and the physical has fallen away. Here, I have one aspect of the human organization. The element of harmony contains the center of my etheric system; again, the physical has fallen away. Then we reach the next octave; again, in the limb system—it is obvious and goes without saying—I find the element that appears as the rhythmic element of music.

How, indeed, does the musical evolution of man proceed? It begins with the experience of the spiritual, the actual presence of the spiritual in tone, in the musical tone structure. The spiritual fades away; man retains the tone structure. Later, he links it with the word, which is a remnant of the spiritual; and what he had earlier as imaginations, namely the instruments, he fashions here in the physical, out of physical substance, as his musical instruments. To the extent that they arouse the musical mood, the instruments are all derived from the spiritual world. When he built physical musical instruments, man simply filled the empty spaces that remained after he no longer beheld the spiritual. Into those spaces he put the physical instruments.

It is correct to say that in music more than anywhere else one can see how the transition to the materialistic age proceeds. In the place where musical instruments resound today, spiritual entities stood formerly. They are gone, they have disappeared from the ancient clairvoyance. If man wishes to take objective hold of the musical element, however, he needs something that does not exist in outer nature. Outer nature offers him no equivalent to the musical element; therefore, he requires musical instruments.

The musical instruments basically are a clear reflection of the fact that music is experienced by the whole human being. The wind instruments prove that the head of man experiences music. The string instruments are living proof that music is experienced in the chest, primarily expressed in the arms. All percussion instruments—or those in between string and percussion instruments—are evidence of how the musical element is expressed in the third part of man's nature, the limb system. Also, however, everything connected with the wind instruments has a more intimate relation to the element of melody than that which is connected with the string instruments,

74

which have a relation to the element of harmony. That which is connected with percussion possesses more inner rhythm and relates to the rhythmic element. An orchestra is an image of man; it must not include a piano, however. Why is that? The musical instruments are derived from the spiritual world; the piano, however, in which the tones are abstractly lined up next to each other, is created only in the physical world by man. All instruments like the flute or violin originate musically from the higher world. A piano is like the Philistine who no longer contains within him the higher human being. The piano is the Philistine instrument. It is fortunate that there is such an instrument, or else the Philistine would have no music at all. The piano arises out of a materialistic experience of music. It is therefore the instrument that can be used most conveniently to evoke the musical element within the material realm. Pure matter was put to use so that the piano could become an expression of the musical element. Naturally, the piano is a beneficial instrument—otherwise, we would have to rely from the beginning on the spiritual in musical instruction in our materialistic age—but it is the one instrument that actually, in a musical sense, must be overcome. Man must get away from the impressions of the piano if he wishes to experience the actual musical element.

It is therefore always a great experience when a composition by an artist who basically lives completely in the element of music, such as Bruckner, is played on the piano. In Bruckner's compositions, the piano seems to disappear from the room! One forgets the piano and thinks that one is hearing other instruments; this is indeed so in Bruckner's case. It proves that something of the essentially spiritual, which lies at the basis of all music, still lived in Bruckner, though in a very instinctive way.

These are the things that I wished to tell you today,

75

though in a fragmentary, informal way. I believe we will soon have an opportunity to continue with these matters. Then, I shall go into more detail concerning this or that aspect.

VII

Recently, I have called attention repeatedly to the fact that, just as one can give a biographical description of man's waking life, so one could offer one of the time spent during sleep. Everything the human being experiences during his waking hours is experienced through his physical and etheric bodies. By virtue of the appropriately developed sense organs in the physical and etheric bodies he is conscious of this world, which, as his environment, is related to the physical and etheric bodies; it is at one with them, so to speak. Since man at his present level of evolution has not similarly developed soul-spiritual organs in his astral body and "I" that would serve as supersensible sense organs—to coin a paradoxical expression— he cannot bring his consciousness into what he experiences between falling asleep and awakening. Only spiritual vision, therefore, could survey that which would be contained in the biography of this "I" and astral body, which runs parallel to the biography that we come to with the help of the physical and the etheric bodies.

If one speaks of man's waking experiences, they necessarily include what, together with him and caused by him, takes place in his physical-etheric environment. One therefore must speak of a physical-etheric environment or world in which man exists during his waking life. Likewise, man is in another world during sleep; this world, however, is totally different from the physical-etheric

77

world. Just as the physical world is our environment when we are awake, so supersensible vision is in a position to speak of a world that surrounds us similarly when we sleep. In this lecture we shall bring before our souls some of the aspects that can illuminate that world. The basic elements for it are described in my book, *An Outline of Occult Science*.[12] There you find described in a certain way, though in a sketchy form, how the realms of the physical-etheric world—the mineral, plant, animal, and human realms—continue upward into the realms of the higher hierarchies. We shall now take a closer look at this.

When, in the waking state, we turn our eyes or other sense organs in the direction of our physical-etheric environment, we perceive the three, or four, realms of nature, namely, the mineral, plant, animal, and human realms. Ascending to those regions that are accessible only to supersensible consciousness, we find a continuation, as it were, of these realms: the realms of the Angeloi, Archangeloi, Archai, Exusiai, Dynamis, Kyriotetes, and so forth (see diagram on page 81).

We therefore have two worlds interpenetrating one another, the physical-etheric world and the supersensible world. We already know that during sleep we are indeed in this supersensible world and have experiences there, despite the fact that, due to the absence of soul-spiritual organs, these experiences do not reach ordinary consciousness.

To arrive at a more specific comprehension of what the human being experiences in this supersensible world, one must describe this world in the same way as one describes the physical-etheric world by means of natural science and history. Regarding the supersensible science that concerns the actual course of events in the world in which we exist as sleeping human beings, we naturally must select particular details to begin with. Today, I shall select one event of profound significance for the whole evolution of humanity in the last few thousand years. We have already discussed this event repeatedly from the viewpoint of the physical-etheric world and its history. Today, we shall discuss it from another viewpoint, that of the supersensible world. The event to which I refer is one that falls in the fourth century A.D.

I have described how the whole composition of human souls in the West becomes different in that century. Without spiritual scientific insight into this matter, one actually no longer understands how human beings sensed and felt before the fourth century A.D. We have frequently described, however, this composition of soul, this feeling. We have described in different words what human beings experienced in the course of that age. Now we shall take a brief glance at what the beings who belong to the supersensible realm experienced during that same time. We shall turn to the other side of life, as it were, and take the viewpoint of the supersensible realm.

It is a prejudice of contemporary, so-called enlightened human beings to believe that their thoughts are confined only to their heads. We would discover nothing of the things around us through thoughts if these thoughts were only within the heads of man. He who believes that thoughts are only in the human head is as prejudiced as one—paradoxical as this might sound—who believes that the drink of water with which he quenches his thirst originated on his tongue instead of flowing into his mouth from the glass of water. It is as ridiculous to claim that thoughts originate in the human head as it is to claim that the drink of water originates in the mouth. Indeed, thoughts are spread out all through the world. Thoughts are forces that dwell in all things. Our organ of thinking is simply something that partakes of the cosmic reservoir of thought forces, absorbing thoughts of itself. We therefore cannot speak of thoughts as if they were the possession only of the human being. Instead, we must be aware that thoughts are world-dominating forces, spread out everywhere in the cosmos. These thoughts, however, do not freely float about, as it were, but are always borne and worked upon by some beings; and, most important, they are not always borne by the same beings.

When we make use of the supersensible world, we find through supersensible research that, up into the fourth century A.D., the thoughts with which human beings made the world comprehensible to themselves were borne outside in the cosmos (I could also say, "they flowed out"—our earthly terms are ill-suited for these sublime occurrences and states of being), that these thoughts were borne or flowed from those hierarchical beings that we designate as the Exusiai or beings of form (see diagram on page 81).

If, out of the science of the mysteries, an ancient Greek wished to give an account of how he actually had acquired his thoughts, he would have had to do it in the following way. He would have said, "I turn my spiritual sight up toward those beings who, through the science of the mysteries, have been revealed to me as the beings of form, the forces or beings of form. They are the bearers of cosmic intelligence, they are the bearers of cosmic thoughts. They let thoughts stream through all the world events, and they bestow these human thoughts upon the soul so that it can experience them consciously." A person who, through a special initiation, had gained access to the supersensible world in those ancient Greek times and had come to experience and behold these form beings, would, in order to form a correct picture, a true imagination of them, have had to attribute to them the thoughts that stream and radiate through the world. As an ancient Greek he beheld how, from their limbs, as it were, these form beings let stream forth radiant thought forces,

80

which then entered the world processes and there continued to be effective as the world-creative powers of intelligence.

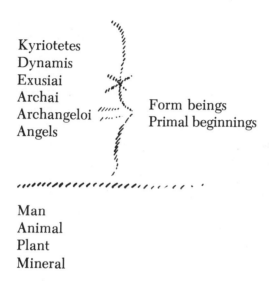

Kyriotetes
Dynamis
Exusiai
Archai
Archangeloi
Angels

Form beings
Primal beginnings

Man
Animal
Plant
Mineral

He thus could say that in the cosmos, the universe, the Exusiai, the forces of form, have the task of pouring thoughts into all the world processes. A material science describes human deeds by noting what people do individually or together. In focusing on the activity of the form forces of that particular age, a supersensible science would have to describe how these supersensible beings let the thought forces stream from one to the other, how they received them from one another, and how, in this streaming and receiving, the world processes are incorporated that appear outwardly to man as natural phenomena.

The evolution of humanity now approached the fourth century A.D. In the supersensible world, thought brought about an extremely significant event; namely, the Exusiai—the forces or beings of form—gave their thought forces up to the Archai, to the primal forces or primal beginnings (see drawing, page 81). The primal beginnings, or Archai, took over the task formerly executed by the Exusiai. Such things happen in the supersensible world. This was a particularly sublime and significant cosmic event. From that time on, the Exusiai, the form beings, retained only the task of regulating the outer sense perceptions, therefore ruling with particular cosmic forces over everything existing in the world of colors, tones, and so forth. Concerning the age that now dawned after the fourth century A.D., a person who can discern these matters must say that he beholds how the world-dominating thoughts are passed on to the Archai, the primal beginnings, how what eyes see and what ears hear, the manifold world phenomena engaged in perpetual metamorphosis, are the tapestry woven by the Exusiai. They formerly bestowed the thoughts on human beings; they now give human beings their sense impressions, while the primal beginnings bestow the thoughts on human beings.

This fact of the supersensible world was mirrored below in the sense world. In the ancient age in which lived the Greek, for example, thoughts were objectively perceived in all things. Just as today we believe that we perceive the color red or blue streaming forth from an object, so the ancient Greek found not only that he grasped a thought with his brain but that the thought streamed forth out of the things, just as red or blue streams forth. In my book, *The Riddles of Philosophy*,[13] I have described the human side, so to speak, of the matter, how this important process of the supersensible world is reflected in the physical-sensible world. There, I employed philosophical expressions, because philosophical terminology is a language for the material world. When one discusses the matter from the viewpoint of the supersensible world, however, one must speak of the supersensible fact that the task of the Exusiai passed on to the Archai.

Such things are prepared in humanity through whole epochs of time and are connected with fundamental changes in human souls. I said that this supersensible event took place in the fourth century A.D., but this is only an approximation, a mean point in time, as it were. This transference of a spiritual task took place over a long period of time. It had been prepared already in pre-Christian times and was completed only in the twelfth, thirteenth, and fourteenth centuries A.D. The fourth century is just the mean century, which is mentioned so as to pinpoint something definite in the historical development of humanity.

This is also the point of time in humanity's evolution when the view of the supersensible world began to vanish completely for man. The consciousness of the soul ceased to see supersensibly, to perceive, because this human soul surrendered itself to the earth. You perhaps will understand this more clearly if we shed light on it from yet another angle.

What is really implied here? What am I trying to point out so intensely? It is the fact that human beings feel themselves more and more in their individuality. As the world of thoughts passes from the form beings to the primal beginnings, from the Exusiai to the Archai, man increasingly senses the thoughts in his own being, because the Archai live one level nearer man than the Exusiai. Now, when man begins to see supersensibly, he has the following impression. He realizes that this [see diagram] is the world that he perceives as the sense world. One side [yellow in the diagram] is turned toward his senses, the other [red] is already hidden from the senses. Ordinary consciousness knows nothing of the relationships that are to be considered here. Supersensible consciousness, on the other hand, has the impression that between man [see diagram] and the sense impressions there are the Angeloi, Archangeloi, and Archai; they are really on this side of the sense world. Though one does not see them with ordinary eyes, they actually are situated between man and the whole tapestry of sense impressions. The Exusiai, Dynamis, and Kyriotetes are actually located beyond this realm; they are concealed by the tapestry of sense impressions.

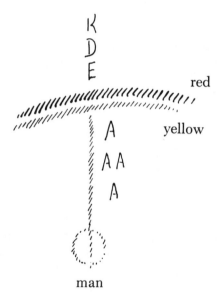

man

A human being having supersensible consciousness senses that the thoughts are coming closer to him since having been given over to the Archai. He senses them as being located more in his world, whereas formerly they were located behind the appearance of things; they approached man, as it were, through the red or blue color, or the tone of c-sharp or g. Since this transference of thoughts, man feels a freer association with the world of thoughts. This also gives rise to the illusion that man himself produces the thoughts.

In the course of time, the human being evolved to the point where he could enclose in himself, as it were, what formerly offered itself to him as objective outer world. This came about only gradually in human evolution. Going back into the distant past of human evolution, to the ancient Atlantean time preceding the Atlantean catastrophe, picture to yourselves the human configuration at that time, as described in my books, *An Outline of Occult Science* or *Cosmic Memory*.[14] As you know, human beings of that time were formed completely differently. The substance of their bodies was more delicate than it became later in the post-Atlantean age. For this reason, the soul element also stood in a different relationship to the world—all this is described in the above books—and these Atlanteans experienced the world completely differently. I just wish to point out one aspect of their particular kind of experience. Atlanteans could not yet experience musical intervals of thirds, not even fifths. Their musical experience really began with feeling the sevenths. They then felt further intervals, of which the seventh was the smallest. They missed hearing thirds and fifths; these intervals did not exist for Atlanteans.

The experience of tone structure was completely different, and the soul had a completely different relationship to the tone structure. One who lives musically only in sevenths, with no intervals in between, as naturally as did the Atlanteans does not even perceive the musical element as something that occurs around or within him. The moment he perceives the musical element he feels transported out of his body into the cosmos. This was the case with the Atlanteans. Their musical experience converged with a direct religious experience. Their experience of the seventh did not make them feel that they themselves had something to do with the appearance of the interval of the seventh. Instead, they sensed how the gods, who pervaded and wove through the world, revealed themselves in sevenths. The statement, "I make music," would have made no sense to them. The only meaningful thing for them to say was, "I live in music made by the gods."

In a much diminished form, this musical experience still existed in the post-Atlantean age during the period when people lived mainly in the interval of the fifth. This must not be compared to man's present-day feeling for the fifth. Today, the fifth gives man an impression of being something external that lacks content. Man experiences something empty in the fifth, though in a positive sense of the word empty. The fifth has become empty because the gods have withdrawn from human beings.

Still, in the post-Atlantean age too, man experienced in the interval of the fifth that the gods actually lived in these fifths. Only later, when the third appeared in the musical element—both major and minor thirds—the musical element submerged itself, as it were, into human feeling [*Gemüt*]; hence, man no longer felt transported from his body while experiencing music. Man was definitely transported in musical life during the true era of the fifth. In the era of thirds, however, which as you know dawned only relatively recently, man is within himself when he experiences music. He brings the musical element close to his corporeality. He interweaves it with his corporeality. Along with the experience of the third, therefore, the difference between major and minor keys arises. Man becomes aware of what can be experienced through the major key on the one hand and the minor key on the other. With the third and the appearance of major and minor keys, the musical experience now links itself with uplifting, joyous human moods and with depressed, sad moods, which the human being experiences as a bearer of his physical and etheric bodies. In a manner of speaking, man withdraws his experience of the world from the cosmos and unites it with himself. Formerly, his most important experience of the world was such—this was definitely still the case in the "fifth-era," if I may put it like this, but much more so in the "seventh-era"—that it directly transported him, that he could say, "The world of tones draws my 'I' and my astral body out of my physical and etheric bodies. I interweave my earthly existence with the divine-spiritual world, and, on the wings of the tone structure, the gods move through the world. I participate in their moving when I perceive the tones."

In this specific area you can see how cosmic experience draws near to man, as it were; how the cosmos penetrates man; how, when we go back to earlier ages, we must seek in the supersensible for the most important human experiences; and how the age is approaching when man as an earthly sense phenomenon must be taken along, as it were, when the most important world events are described. This occurs in the age before which the dominion over thoughts passed from the form beings to the primal beginnings. This is also reflected in the fact that the ancient "fifth-era," which preceded the above cosmic event, passes on to the "era of thirds" and the experience of major and minor modes.

It is of special interest regarding man's musical experience to go back into a still earlier time, an age of human earthly evolution reaching back into the dimmest primeval past, which can be brought into view by supersensible vision. We arrive at an age—you find it described as the "Lemurian Age" in my *Occult Science*—in which generally man cannot perceive the musical element that can become conscious in him in an interval within one octave. In that age, man perceives only an interval that surpasses one octave:

c d e f g a b c d

He perceives only the above interval c to d above c^1. In the Lemurian age we discover a musical experience that excludes hearing any interval within one octave; the interval instead reaches to the first tone of the following octave, and on to the second tone—the e—of the next higher octave. It is difficult to put into words what the human being experienced then, but perhaps one can form an idea of it if I say that Lemurian man experienced the second of the next higher and the third of the second higher octave. He experienced a kind of objective third, and there he also experienced both major and minor thirds. It is not a third in our sense, of course, because one has an actual third only when I take the prime in the same octave and the tone that I refer to as being the second-nearest to the prime. Because ancient man was able to experience such intervals, however—we would say today, prime in the first octave, second in the next, third in the third octave—he perceived something like an objective major and minor mode, not one experienced within himself but one that was felt to be an expression of the soul experiences of the gods. One cannot say that Lemurians experienced joy and suffering, exaltation and depression, but one must say that, due to the particular musical sensation of the Lemurian age, when, in a completely transported state, human beings perceived these intervals, they experienced the god's cosmic sounds of joy and lamentation. We thus can look back upon an epoch of the earth actually experienced by human beings when what man experiences today in major and minor modes was projected, so to speak, into the universe. What today he experiences inwardly was once projected out into the universe. What today wells up in his life of feeling [*Gemüt*], in his sensation, he perceived—transported from his physical body— as the experience of the gods. Our present inner experience of a major musical mood was perceived by Lemurian man, when he was transported from his physical body, as the cosmic song of jubilation, as the cosmic music of jubilation, produced by the gods as an expression of joy over their world creation. What today we know as an inner minor mood experience, man perceived in the Lemurian age as the overwhelming lamentation of the gods concerning the possibility that humanity could fall victim to what subsequently has been described by the Bible as the fall into sin, the falling away from the benevolent divine-spiritual powers.

This is something that sounds forth to us from the wonderful knowledge of the ancient mysteries, which at the same time was in itself artistic; it is not an abstract description of how humanity once passed through the Luciferic and Ahrimanic seduction and temptation and experienced such and such a thing. Human beings actually heard how, in primeval times, the gods made jubilant music in the cosmos because they rejoiced over their cosmic creativity. They also heard how the gods prophetically envisioned man's fall from the divine-spiritual powers and brought this to expression in their cosmic lamentation. This knowledge, which later took on increasingly intellectual forms, resounds as an artistic conception from the ancient mysteries. From this we can gain the profound conviction that it was only a single source from which flowed knowledge, art, and religion. From this the conviction must grow in us that we must return to that human soul composition, and it will arise again if the soul perceives [*erkennt*], through the religious welling up in it, the artistic streaming through it. Such a composition of soul will understand vividly once again what Goethe meant when he said, "Beauty is a manifestation of secret natural laws without which these phenomena would have remained forever hidden." The secret of human evolution within earthly existence, within earthly becoming, betrays itself to us by this inner unity of everything that man, perceiving religiously and artistically, must go through with the world, so that along with the world he can experience his entire development.

The time has come when man must become conscious again of these matters, because otherwise the soul qualities of human nature will simply deteriorate. Through the increasingly intellectual, one-sided form of knowledge, man of today and the immediate future would have to become arid in his soul; the arts, grown one-sided, would dull his soul; and one-sided religion would drain him of his soul altogether, if he were unable to find the path that could lead him to an inner harmony and union of these three; if he could not find the way to rise out of himself— in a more conscious way than was formerly the case—and once again to see and hear the supersensible together with the sense world.

When, with the aid of the science of the spirit, one looks back at the ancient, great personalities of the dawning Greek culture, whose descendants were men like Aeschylus or Heraklitus, one finds that, in so far as they were initiated into the mysteries, these personalities all had the same feeling born out of their knowledge and their artistic forces of creativity. They felt their artistic creativity just as Homer did, who said, "Sing, O Muse, to me of the wrath of Achilles," not as something personal pervading them but as something they accomplished in their religious experience in community with the spiritual world. It motivated them to say the following: in primeval times, human beings actually experienced themselves as human beings by withdrawing from themselves during their most important human activities—I explained to you that this was in the case of music, but it was like this also in forming thoughts—and communing with the gods. Human beings have lost what they thus experienced. This mood of the loss of an ancient cognitive, artistic, and religious treasure of humanity weighed heavily on the deeper Greek souls.

Another mood must come over modern man. By unfolding the appropriate forces of his soul experience he must reach the point where he rediscovers what once was lost. I would like to put it like this: man must develop a consciousness—after all, we live in the age of consciousness—of how that which has become inward can once again find the way out to the divine-spiritual. In *one* realm, for example, this will be accomplished when the inner wealth of feeling experienced in a melody one day will be discovered in the single tone, at which time the secret of individual tone will be experienced by man. In other words, man not only will experience intervals but will be able to experience the single tone with the same inner richness and inner variation of experience that he can experience today with melody. As yet, today, man can hardly imagine what this will be like.

You see, however, how matters proceed from the seventh to the fifth, from the fifth to the third, and from the third down to the prime, the single tone, and so forth. What was once the loss of the divine must transform itself for human evolution if humanity on earth is not to perish but to continue its development. The loss must transform itself for earthly humanity into a rediscovery of the divine.

We understand the past correctly only if we are able to confront it with the right image for our evolution in the future; if deeply, deeply shaken we are able to feel what a profound person could feel in ancient Greek times, "I have lost the presence of the gods"; if, with a shaken but intensely and warmly striving soul, we are able to counter this with the resolve, "We shall bring the spirit that is within us like a seed to blossoming and fruition so that we can find the gods once again!"

Translator's Notes

1. Rudolf Steiner distinguishes here between the sentient *body*, which is the container, as it were, and the actual individualized human soul, the content. The latter consists of sentient soul, intellectual soul, and consciousness soul. See *Theosophy* by Rudolf Steiner for details. Frequently the term "sentient body" refers both to the container and the content.
2. Manas (spirit self), Buddhi (life spirit), and Atma (spirit man) are still-higher members of man's organization that come into being as man's "I" works consciously on the purification and transformation of astral (sentient) body, etheric body, and physical body. Sentient soul, intellectual soul, and consciousness soul were prepared by man's "I" in an unconscious state.
3. A note in the German edition states that a brief description followed here concerning the various members of the human organization but that the transcript was too poor to be reproduced. They were similar to those given in Steiner's *Theosophy* in the chapter "The Being of Man." In particular, the separation of the astral body into sentient body and sentient soul was emphasized.
4. Refers to Rudolf Steiner's lectures, *Man and the World of the Stars/The Spiritual Communion of Man*, Anthroposophic Press, Spring Valley, N.Y., 1982.
5. Rudolf Steiner, *Knowledge of the Higher Worlds and Its Attainment*.

6. The two artists and the concert refer to the recital by the sisters Svardstrom in the Goetheanum at that time.
7. Edward von Hanslick (1825–1904), music critic and author in Vienna. His book, *The Beautiful in Music* (trans. Gustav Cohen, Indianapolis: Bobbs-Merrill, 1957), first appeared in 1854.
8. Contra-tones are the tones below contra-c:

9. The great octave refers to the tones between c^3 and c^2 below middle c.
10. In the following passages, *Vorstellen*, the forming of mental images, or the lower aspect of thinking, has been translated *thinking*, in its relationship to feeling and willing.
11. Rudolf Steiner, *Theosophy*, Anthroposophic Press, Spring Valley, N.Y., 1971.
12. Rudolf Steiner, *An Outline of Occult Science*, Anthroposophic Press, Spring Valley, N.Y., 1972.
13. Rudolf Steiner, *The Riddles of Philosophy*, Anthroposophic Press, Spring Valley, N.Y., 1973.
14. Rudolf Steiner, *Cosmic Memory*, Harper & Rowe, New York, 1981.

Editor's Note

In any translation, of course, decisions must be made concerning whether or how much of the *mood* of the original language need be sacrificed to provide a readable rendition of the ideas. In these lectures, particularly the four later lectures, the almost ethereal mood is very much enhanced by the flexibility of the German language, which permits qualities and essences to be spoken of as things, transforming adjectives into nouns: "*das Musikalische*," literally, "the musical," or "*das Vokalische*" and "*das Konsonantische*," pertaining to the quality of vowels and consonants. Rarely in these lectures does Steiner harden these qualities into substances, into "music," "vowels," "consonants." Unfortunately, the English language is not nearly so flexible in this respect; in translating, the choice must be made either to perform the hardening that Steiner avoided or to juggle a rather cumbersome series of phrases—"the musical element," "the element of the vowel," and so on. While graceful prose is more difficult with these phrases, the choice nevertheless has been made to use them in an attempt to preserve the quality of the original.

Publisher's Note

The lectures printed here were given by Rudolf Steiner to audiences familiar with the general background and terminology of his anthroposophical teaching. It should be remembered that in his autobiography, *The Course of My Life*, he emphasizes the distinction between his written works on the one hand, and on the other, reports of lectures that were given as oral communications and were not originally intended for print. For an intelligent appreciation of the lectures it should be borne in mind that certain premises were taken for granted when the words were spoken. "These premises," Rudolf Steiner writes, "include at the very least the anthroposophical knowledge of Man and of the Cosmos in its spiritual essence; also what may be called 'anthroposophical history,' told as an outcome of research into the spiritual world."

RECOVERING THE SOURCES OF MEANING:
THE PATH OF ANTHROPOSOPHY

Anthroposophy is not just an abstract philosophy but a living spiritual path that reconnects human beings to the universe and to the sources of what it means to be human. Rudolf Steiner, who renewed this path of meaning in our time, saw four of his books as fundamental to the recovery of human dignity. Despite the many other books he wrote, and the more than 6,000 lectures he gave, Steiner returned again and again to these four basic books.

The Philosophy of Spiritual Activity

This fundamental work of philosophy demonstrates the fact of freedom. Read properly, the book leads the reader to experience the living thinking by which all human activity may be renewed.

Knowledge of the Higher Worlds and its Attainment

This fundamental guide to the anthroposophical path of knowledge. Steiner details the exercises and moral qualities to be cultivated on the path to conscious experience of super- sensible realities.

Theosophy

This work begins by describing the threefold nature of the human being. A profound discussion of reincarnation and karma follows, concluding with a description of the soul's journey through the supersensible regions after death.

An Outline of Occult Science

This masterwork places humanity at the heart of the vast, invisible processes of cosmic evolution. Descriptions of the different members of tthe human being, are followed by a profound investigation of cosmic evolution .